PERFECTING THE SAINTS

God's Blueprint For Getting The Whole Church Working

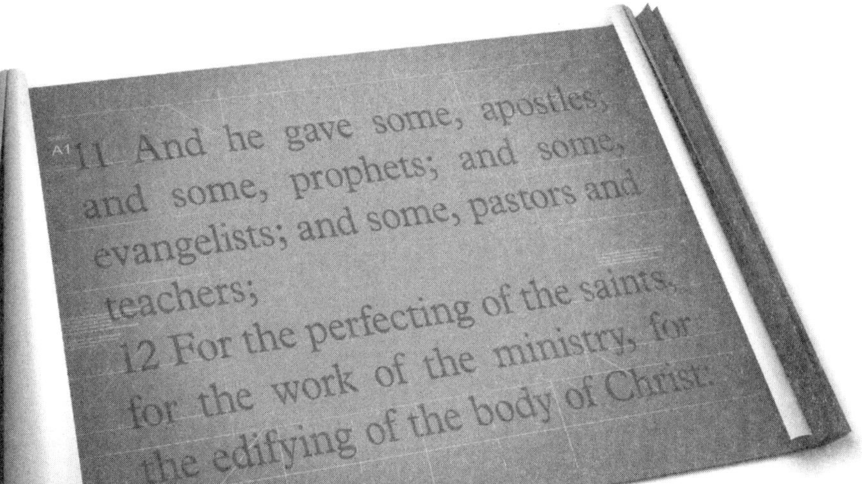

DR. JAMES WILKINS

Writings contained herein are by the author unless otherwise stated.

Printed in the United States of America.

All Scriptures are taken from the King James Bible.

ISBN # 978-1-61119-082-3

Printed by Calvary Publishing
A Ministry of Parker Memorial Baptist Church
1902 East Cavanaugh Road, Lansing, Michigan 48910
www.CalvaryPublishing.org

CP KJV
Calvary PUBLISHING
FOR BAPTISTS BY BAPTISTS
A ministry of Parker Memorial Baptist Church
1902 East Cavanaugh Road • Lansing, Michigan 48910
Phone: 517.882.2112 • Fax: 517.882.2317
www.calvarypublishing.org

Table of Contents

Foreword

When Jesus came from outer space (Heaven) in order to pay for men's sins, He had to **develop a way** to get His message of love and salvation to every man on earth.

In order to do so He had to have a home base so **He organized His first local church.**

He had to develop trained workers that knew His message of love and salvation well enough **to train others**.

This meant He had to **have a method of training** which would do more than teach their convert about Him and His Word (doctrine). He needed a method which would train others well enough so they could tell others about His love and the wonderful plan of salvation **as well as train them to carry that message to every creature in the world.** That method had to include a way to **reach rapid growth** because the world's population was growing rapidly.

This method of training had to be simple because every child of God, both members and pastors, **were supposed to do it.**

Please bear in mind that Jesus had to come to earth and pay for man's sins because man was already under the sentence of eternal death (separation from God). In order for man to be saved **he must hear and accept God's offer of salvation** through the sacrificial death and payment of His Son.

Please bear in mind that the suffering and death of Jesus on the cross is **absolutely useless** to people unless they hear and act upon it. They are already condemned and will spend eternity in Hell unless they hear and are persuaded to accept Jesus as their personal Saviour.

The question arises, what method of training is **both simple and still leads to rapid expansion** throughout the world?

The best and simplest Scripture which reveals this marvelous method of training is Acts 20:20.

Paul first states, "...how I kept back nothing that was profitable *unto you...*" This statement means he was fully committed to their training.

His second statement reveals the actual simple method of training, "...but have **shewed you,** and have **taught you publickly,** and from house to house."

Paul would show the members how to approach the sinner and deal with helping them understand their sinful, lost condition and then reveal how to receive Jesus as their Saviour by faith. **Then he would walk through the procedure with someone who was posing as a sinner and demonstrate how to get him to pray and accept the Saviour.** He would continue doing this publicly before giving them **on the job training** by showing and teaching them from house to house. He would continue this showing and teaching them publicly and by giving them on the job training until **they were perfected to train others.**

This new trainee would become a soul-winning trainer and now there were two soul-winning, training teams. It is very obvious from reading the book of Acts that this simple method of training soon had training teams who were reproducing themselves all over the earth.

Remember, time does not alter this principle. This simple plan of developing trained workers which worked so wonderfully well in the Bible days will work in our day if we can find Christians **who love the Lord well enough to work it.**

Perfecting the Saints will be a blueprint for developing these trained workers.

We have had revivals back in America's history which were started by:

- Strong, spirit filled preaching that had a good method of involving its members.
- Prayer meetings which spread all over the country.

The book of Acts revivals included prayer, sprit filled preaching and a good method of involving all the members through the book of Acts with on-the-job training.

My prayer is – **let us return back to the book of Acts method of training** and have a nation-changing revival!

"...how I kept back nothing that was profitable *unto you*[total commitment by the pastors] but have shewed you, and have taught you publickly, and [on-the-job-training] from house to house," Acts 20:20

PERSONAL GROWTH SEMINAR

A month long saturation which goes beyond convincing and convicting…

It converts

This seminar includes:

- Two sessions per night in which the material is clearly presented and demonstrated.
- Two people are assigned to work with and help each other during the month.
- Prepared notes are provided for all.
- Participants are motivated to study 30 minutes each day.
- Sunday school material is provided to strengthen the principles taught.
- Family devotional material designed for daily use.
- Textbook prepared especially for the seminar.
- C.D.'s of all sessions of the seminar.

HITS THE GOAL

"PERFECTING THE SAINTS"

SCRIPTURAL FOUNDATION FOR THE PERSONAL GROWTH SEMINAR

"...being seen of them [apostles] forty days, and speaking of the things pertaining to the kingdom of God:" Acts 1:3

This month long series of studies is based on the principle of saturation, which Jesus used to convert the apostles from non-motivated disciples (I go a fishing) to flaming evangelists who could not be stopped.

Jesus spent forty days with the apostles in which He spoke of nothing but the Kingdom (millennial reign and their future place in it).

The principle of saturation and its benefits upon the people who submit to it is vividly stated in Psalm 1:1-3:

"*Blessed* is the man that walketh not in the counsel of the ungodly, nor standeth in the way of sinners, nor sitteth in the seat of the scornful. But his delight is in the law of the LORD; and in his law doth he meditate day and night. And he shall be like a tree planted by the rivers of water, that bringeth forth his fruit in his season; his leaf also shall not wither; and whatsoever he doeth shall prosper."

It is the same principle of saturation which churches have used to convert and strengthen their members in stewardship, giving and *Faith Promise Missions*.

The saturation principle is in harmony with how the brain works. The brain first:

1. Hears a truth and believes it.
2. Then studies (meditates) on that truth until it becomes a conviction (they believe it).
3. The brain continues to meditate and absorb the truth until it passes through the stages of belief and conviction into the subconscious of man to become part of that man which directs his life. It becomes not just a thought or something he believes, but it becomes part of him and defines who he is and how he will live.

The benefit one receives from the Personal Growth Seminar can be best illustrated by Grandma's cat.

Grandma was using an old fashioned wooden churn to churn butter. While churning butter out on the back porch her cat was asleep on a ledge above

Grandma's rocking chair. Just as Grandma opened the mouth of the churn to inspect the butter and see if it was made, Rover, the dog, let out a loud bark which frightened the sleeping cat that then sprang to land on the safety of Grandma's shoulder. As Grandma leaned forward the cat missed her shoulder, landing in the open churn. Grandma fished around in the buttermilk until she found the tail of the cat. She then proceeded to pull the cat out of the churn by the tail with one hand while squeezing the buttermilk off of the cat with the other hand saying, "You didn't put nothing in and you ain't going to take nothing out."

You will only take out of this life changing seminar what you put into it!

Put a lot in...get a lot back. Put a little in and continue to struggle as a believer.

INTRODUCING THE PERSONAL GROWTH SEMINAR

The *Personal Growth Seminar* is a month long directed study for self-improvement.

Principles will be given and demonstrated each week for the student to work on for a minimum of 30 minutes each day.

Prepared notes for each lecture will be given to each student. The average retention of each lesson when read one time is **6%**. If the notes are read 6 consecutive days, this retention increases to **62%**.

We will give you Directed Studies which will enable the participants to develop skill in the following areas:

- How to develop better relationships with **friends**, **family** and **church members**.
- How to overcome **visitation fright**, insecurities and an **inferiority complex**.
- How to develop c**onversational poise** and a more positive outlook toward life.
- How to have c**onfidence** and to **properly share one's faith.**
- How to recognize and overcome **attacks of the Devil**.
- How to live a more c**onsistent life** – free of excessive emotional highs and lows.
- How to understand oneself and **live a more fruitful, satisfying life.**

PERSONAL GROWTH SEMINAR

IS MORE THAN A SOUL-WINNING SEMINAR

Helps the LAYMAN:

- Accept his personal responsibility to witness.
- Understand his source of fear and how to overcome it.
- Break through the barrier of awkwardness so he can witness with confidence.
- Establish the Biblical pattern of Soul-Winner Trainer – Silent Partner-Trainee.
- Rekindle new vision and hope.

CONVERTS – To a New Way of Life...THE ABUNDANT LIFE!

RECOMMENDATIONS AND TESTIMONIES CONCERNING THE PERSONAL GROWTH SEMINAR

SOME FULL STATEMENTS FROM LAYMEN:

Brother Wilkins, I praise God for revealing through you my true purpose in life. It has given me a new vision of my responsibilities to my Saviour and God. I KNOW BECAUSE OF THIS SEMINAR I WILL NEVER BE THE SAME. God bless you. – In love, Bro. Bob Sanford.

Brother Wilkins, Not counting the day I was saved (which was and always will be the greatest thing that has ever happened to me) this series of lessons on soul-winning HAS BEEN GREAT AND A REAL BLESSING. IT HAS CHANGED MY WHOLE CHRISTIAN LIFE. I knew the Bible told us to be soul-winners and people for years have told us how, but NOBODY BEFORE HAS EVER MADE IT SO PLAIN THAT I COULD REALLY SEE AND KNOW THE WAY TO GO ABOUT IT. May God really bless you and continue to use you to shed light on soul-winning for other Christians. – Mrs. Little

Brother Wilkins, I thought this was the best THAT HAS EVER HAPPENED TO ME AND THE GREATEST EXPERIENCE. It has really helped me to not just go ON VISITATION BUT TO GO SOUL-WINNING. I'D RECOMMEND THIS COURSE TO EVERYONE I KNOW. I'll pray that God will continue to use and bless you always. Maybe because of what you have taught us, we may keep some lost soul from going to hell. Thank you, - Betty T.

Dr. Wilkins, Brother Wilkins, besides my preacher, Brother Cheek, you have greatly influenced my life. I WAS SINCERELY SEARCHING A REASON WHY I TRULY EXIST. I'm full of the true joy and life now, knowing I'm meant to be a successful soul-winner. I could not express in mere words the joy that floods my heart from applying these methods to a lost soul. Thank you – I am alive. – Yours in Christ – Trudy Thomason

SOME FULL STATEMENTS FROM PASTORS:

Praise God for this seminar. It has not only CHALLENGED MY PEOPLE BUT HAS EQUIPPED THEM TO DO WHAT GOD SAVED THEM TO DO, TO WIN SOULS. It is entirely Scriptural, and I heartily recommend it to all Pastors and churches everywhere. – **Bob Cheek, Pastor**

The principles which are learned in the Personal Growth Seminar helped our church tremendously. We averaged over 70 out for Soul-Winning Visitation ever week in July. – **Marvin Weido, Pastor**

Dr. Wilkins directed and taught a soul-winning clinic here at Castleberry Baptist Church. Already we are witnessing our people winning people to the Lord. He will be a blessing to any church and pastor in his preaching or in a soul-winning clinic. My prayer is that many will invite him to come. – **Dr. Scotty Alexander – Fort Worth, Texas**

The Personal Growth Seminar is the best meeting that I ever attended. It helped my people more than anything I have ever taken them to. – **Ed Johnson, Bluffton, Indiana**

Dr. Wilkins, The soul-winning seminars have been one of the greatest blessings of my life. I've sat under Dr. Hyles, Robinson, Westmoreland and others but Dr. Wilkins, you got down close to what I needed to get me out winning souls. The lectures are so spirit filled they reach the heart. I have no suggestions to improve them whatsoever. You may be sure that souls will be saved because I sat in these classes. – **David Piearcy, Pastor**

SOME WHO WON SOULS FOR THE FIRST TIME:

I have learned to witness and be a soul-winner with confidence. – **G.J.**

It has given me a totally different outlook toward my CHRISTIAN ABILITIES. I am no longer frightened of the devil and his fiery darts and I am learning how to combat his fiery darts. – **D.H.**

Realizing the methods of the devil has helped me greatly. This was the greatest hindrance to me in previous visits and now I can effectively contend with it. – **Charles Morris**

The Abundant Life Seminar is one of the most exciting programs that I have ever been a part of. Dr. Wilkins has many tremendous insights in dealing with people about Christ. For the first time in a long time, visiting is exciting to me. THE FEELING IS TREMENDOUS WHEN YOU KNOW HOW TO DEFEAT SATAN ON EVERY SINGLE VISIT. PRAISE GOD FOR THIS SEMINAR. – Tim Hodges

Brother Wilkins, This seminar has been a tremendous blessing to me and my life. I seem to have had only a semi-burden for lost souls, but now my heart is open to those souls. I've made a commitment to be a soul-winner and to keep my eyes on the Lord for strength." I'VE ALWAYS HAD SUCH A PROBLEM WITH INFERIORITY AND A POOR SELF-IMAGE AND YOUR TALKS HAVE REALLY HELPED IN THIS WAY. THE DEVIL WOULD LIKE TO DESTROY ME IN THIS WAY, BUT I'M DETERMINED HE WON'T. I'm praying for you and your ministry. I do believe our churches need this program!– Mrs. Diana Blondeau

SOME TEENS WROTE:

"This course has helped me tremendously in my home life."

"I hurt and broke my parent's hearts for the last time. Please don't tell my parents...I quit smoking pot."

THE SENTIMENTS OF SO MANY:

"I wish I could have had this course when I was first saved. I have always wanted to win someone to the Lord but I was afraid. Thank you for this class. I know with the Lord's help I can do it."

"You made me admit I didn't care – you changed my life completely."

"If you are already a soul-winner, it will make your efforts much easier. If you are not a soul-winner, you will be at the end of the six-week course."

Director's Note: These recommendations are several years old but time does not alter truth. As we have new seminars we will have many more, and I believe, much more exciting recommendations.

MY PASTOR'S ENDORSEMENT

October 3, 2012

To Whom It May Concern:

THE "PERSONAL GROWTH SEMINAR" WRITTEN AND PRESENTED BY DR. JAMES WILKINS IS FABULOUS. Recently Dr. Wilkins trained many of the people of Valley Bible Baptist Church in the principles of effective soul-winning using his "Personal Growth Seminar." The training consisted of five consecutive Thursday evening sessions beginning on Thursday, August 9, 2012, and ending Thursday, September 6, 2012. In addition to the Thursday evening sessions, Dr. Wilkins taught the adult Sunday school class on Sunday mornings and concluded the seminar on Sunday night, September 9, by preaching his message entitled, "The Call of a Lost and Dying World."

Valley Bible Baptist Church is still experiencing fruit from the seminar. A total of 68 people graduated from the "Personal Growth Seminar." Many of these have won souls to the Lord both during and since the seminar. Many have committed to the church visitation program as a result of the training. Both the Thursday night and Saturday morning visitation and soul-winning attendance have increased tremendously. Several of those that completed the training are now training others through the church soul-winning/visitation program.

I HIGHLY RECOMMEND DR. WILKINS AND THE "PERSONAL GROWTH SEMINAR" TO ANY CHURCH. Those going through the seminar will gain new confidence in leading others to Christ. They will become stronger Christians and a greater blessing in their service to Christ.

Sincerely,

Brian McMath, Pastor

Valley Bible Baptist Church

Espanola, NM

-Introduction-

Lecture One
Teach Them to Observe (or Do)

Memory Verse

"Study to shew thyself approved unto God, a **workman** that needeth not to be ashamed, rightly dividing the word of truth."
II Timothy 2:15

Introduction: The first lesson, **Teach Them to Observe (or Do)**, is the foundation upon which the following four lessons rest. This is the reason that we ask the pastor to pair people in teams of two. One member should be a mature worker and serve as captain while the other could be younger.

Note the memory verse. The reason one should study is to become a **workman**.

Many quote verse 20, "Teaching them all things whatsoever I have commanded you." If they do not quote it that way, they interpret and believe it that way – **WRONG!** The verse states, "Teaching them to observe all things..." **"Observe"** means to do, to practice, literally, teach them (converts)to "do all things whatsoever I have commanded you.

Lecture One

Teach Them to Observe (or Do)

I. **TO WHOM WAS JESUS SPEAKING?**

a. TO A LOCAL BODY OF BELIEVERS

i. My personal convictions: Jesus formed a church during His personal ministry. To this church He gave the commission to evangelize, to baptize, to teach, and to observe. There are many other organizations who are winning people, and we honestly praise God for every soul they win, but we believe the Bible teaches that Jesus set up a plan to develop, direct, and evangelize communities. HIS PLAN: Evangelize the community through local churches.

ii. The point to grasp: Jesus was talking to believers.

iii. He was not limiting himself to "just preachers"

iv. Settle this point in your mind. Was Jesus speaking to "just preachers" in these verses or to laymen as well? The church is MADE UP OF BELIEVERS, and believers are TO WIN SOULS.

b. JESUS, OUR GREAT EXAMPLE

i. Acts 1–Jesus began both TO DO and TO TEACH. The doing came before the teaching.

ii. Jesus strongly denounced the Scribes and Pharisees as hypocrites because "...they say, and do not" (Matthew 23:3). He said, "this people draweth nigh unto me with their mouth, and honoureth me with *their* lips; but their heart is far from me (Matthew 15:8) Then He denounced them as hypocrites.

iii. He said, "Even as the Son of man came not to be ministered unto but to minister..." (Matthew 20:28). Then He said "...but whosoever will be great among you, let him be your minister;" (Matthew 20:26)

c. TWO VITAL RESPONSIBILITIES TAUGHT IN THESE VERSES

   i. Make disciples, that is, win souls.
   ii. Teach them *to observe all things*.
   iii. Literally, you, the saved, born-again believers, are charged with the task of winning souls <u>and</u> teaching others to win souls.

II. **YOUR PERSONAL COMMISSION TO TEACH OTHERS**

a. STATED IN MATTHEW 28:20 IS – "TEACHING THEM TO OBSERVE..."

b. II TIMOTHY 2:2 REVEALS A PERSONAL, REVOLVING COMMISSION WHICH HAS FINALLY REACHED <u>YOU</u>! "And the things that thou (Timothy) hast heard of me (Apostle Paul) among many witnesses (preachers?), the same commit thou to faithful men (preachers?) who shall be able to teach others also."

   i. There are four responsible teachers in this verse:

      1. Paul taught Timothy.
      2. Timothy taught faithful men.
      3. Faithful men taught others.
      4. Others are to teach others.

ii. What were the others to do? It is inferred that they should begin the circle of teaching all over again. This revolving circle of one generation teaching another generation has finally reached YOU!

c. PETER COMMANDED THE BELIEVER TO SANCTIFYTHE PRINCIPLE OF SOUL-WINNING (I Peter 3:15)

SANCTIFY means "set apart" – master – get a hold of.

i. WHAT? THE LORD GOD IN YOUR HEARTS – This means to know the plan of salvation. Master the plan of salvation, the principles of salvation so you may...
ii. WHY? GIVE AN ANSWER...
iii. TO WHOM? EVERY MAN...
iv. OF WHAT? THE HOPE YOU HAVE...
v. HOW?WITH MEEKNESS and FEAR. You cannot escape your responsibility simply because you are fearful or scared.

d. YOU ARE TO BECOME A TEACHER.
i. Hebrews 5:12, "For the time you ought to be **teachers**..."
ii. If you don't you incur the displeasure of God by drawing back (Hebrews 10:39). Which will you do? Believe to the saving of your life or drawback to perdition or destruction?

III. **THE ONES WHO ARE RESPONSIBLE FOR TEACHING AND DEVELOPING YOU** – The local church was created for this important task of developing those they win, but the Bible is very specific concerning who is to develop the members and how.

a. WHO IS RESPONSIBLE FOR DEVELOPING THE MEMBERS? In Ephesians 4:11 the Bible declares that God gave preachers to the local church in order to develop the membership.
    i. NOTE: Evangelists – pastors – teachers (ministerial gifts)
    ii. Why? For the PERFECTING OF THE SAINTS (Verse 12).
        1. PERFECTING – equipping – developing – training – bringing to maturity
        2. Who? SAINTS. You are either a saint or you "ain't" (SAVED or NOT SAVED).
    iii. For the WORK OF THE MINISTRY
        1. First, the saints are to win souls.
        2. Secondly, the saints are to teach them to observe or do all things.
    iv. The preachers are to train the members to the place where they have a high level (perfecting) or efficiency in soul-winning.
b. HOW ARE THE PREACHERS TO DEVELOP THE MEMBERSHIP IN SOUL-WINNING? They are to teach and develop by way of their example.
    i. Jesus began both to do and to teach.
    ii. In this important task, the pastors are to be examples – I Peter 5:3, "...Being ensamples to the flock." They are over the flock. (Acts 20:28)
    iii. The membership is to submit to the pastor's example, leadership, and training. Hebrews 13:7, "...whose faith follow, considering the end

of *their* conversation [life]." Hebrews 13:17, "Obey them that have the rule over you, and submit yourselves..."

c. HOW DID THE APOSTLE PAUL DEVELOP GREAT SOUL-WINNING CHURCHES?

   i. The Apostle Paul would go into a city which was totally heathen, stay a few weeks, and up to three years, and then leave behind a sound, highly trained, self-supporting church. This church was generally large in membership with pastors and deacons, and would continue on in a scriptural way even after the apostle left. (BUT HOW DID HE DO IT?)

      1. Many just ignore the question by saying, "Well, it happened and you can't deny that," and then drop the subject.
      2. Others say he did it by superhuman, apostolic gifts. The only problem with this reasoning is the statement which Paul made concerning the purpose for which he was saved. Paul said that God saved him so he would become a PATTERN FOR THOSE WHO WOULD HEREAFTER BE SAVED (I Timothy 1:16). If God saved Paul to be a pattern for us, then He would not nullify the purpose for which He saved Paul by giving him special gifts by which he did his great work for God which we do not have.
      3. The Third reaction to this question, "How did Paul do it?", is to examine the

method by which Paul did it order to duplicate the same works.

ii. Paul used a sure-fire method which produced great results. Paul's method will still produce great results today. His method was so simple that most overlook it completely. Note these principles of Paul's success.

1. He traveled with four to ten other preachers Titus, Timothy Dr. Luke and others who worked under Paul's direction doing the same work Paul did. (Acts 20:4) This point is very important in the rapid duplication of Paul's ministry.
2. Acts 20:20 shows the simple method of Paul's success.

a. Paul taught people how to witness in a public meeting.
b. He showed people how to witness in a public service (a soul-winning demonstration).
c. He taught a person how to witness in a home. He was a teacher-example to the young convert while out winning souls. (On-the- Job Training).
d. He would do this until his student had learned sufficiently; then the student would in turn become a teacher. Paul would take a new student and develop him using the same procedure. If the student was slower, Paul took more

time. If the student learned rapidly, Paul took less time. This on-the-job training of showing and teaching until the person is able to win souls and then become a soul-winner-trainer himself will work today.

e. If Paul taught ten men at a time on-the-job training. If Silas would teach ten, if Timothy would teach ten, if Dr. Luke would teach ten, if others taught ten, in a few months Paul and his staff would train fifty to one hundred men who would become trainers. This procedure would then double with Paul and his staff training a new group while the trainees who became trainers would train others. This procedure was followed until the city was evangelized.

IV. JESUS LEFT TWO LINGERING TRUTHS

a. Just before Jesus returned to heaven He left two vivid truths in the minds of His disciples.
    i. The warning that He would come back from heaven at any moment.
    ii. Each servant would have to give account of his life at His return.

Please take time to read and study Luke 12:40-48. Please accept this strong statement of his imminent coming in Luke 12:40 "Be ye therefore ready also: for the Son of man cometh at an hour when ye think not."

iii. The servant who believed IN HIS HEART that Jesus would not come back (soon) became self-centered and carnal and was severely punished at the return of Christ. (v.47)

iv. The servant who knew his Lord's will AND PREPARED NOT HIMSELF, "shall be beaten with many stripes."

v. We need to consider that we are very near to that day when each **one of us will stand before his Lord.**

SUMMARY: The Bible teaches method as strongly as it teaches doctrine. Why limit the beautiful doctrine of God's Word by missing the method of mass evangelism. Pastors and evangelists were given to the saints in order to develop them (by example) in the ministry of winning souls, and training those who are won to win souls. This is done through trainer and silent partner-trainee teams. If we will get back to the New Testament methods, we will have New Testament (Book of Acts) results.

THE CHURCH IS MADE UP OF ____________________ AND BELIEVERS ARE TO ______________SOULS.

JESUS STRONGLY DENOUNCED THE SCRIBES AND PHARISEES AS ________________ BECAUSE "THEY__________ AND ______________ NOT."

YOU, THE BELIEVER, ARE CHARGED WITH NOT ONLY THE TASK OF ______________ SOULS BUT WITH THE ____________________ OF __________________ OTHERS TO WIN SOULS.

4. II TIMOTHY 2:2 REVEALS A ____________________, REVOLVING COMMISSION WHICH HAS FINALLY REACHED ____________________.
5. PETER SAID TO SANCTIFY THE LORD GOD IN YOUR HEARTS: SANCTIFY MEANS____________ APART, ________________, GET ____________________ OF.
6. EVANGELISTS, ________________, AND TEACHERS WERE GIVEN TO ____________________ THE SAINTS. PERFECT MEANS ________________, DEVELOPING, TRAINING, BRINGING TO ______________.
7. THE WORK OF THE MINISTRY MEANS THAT FIRST THE ________________ ARE TO WIN____________ THEN TEACH THEM TO OBSERVE OR ________________ ALL THINGS.
8. THE MEMBERSHIP IS TO ____________________ TO THE PASTOR'S ____________________ OF LEADERSHIP AND ____________________. (HEBREWS 13:17)
9. PAUL ______________________ PEOPLE HOW TO WITNESS IN A PUBLIC ____________________. HE ______________________ PEOPLE HOW TO WITNESS IN A ______________________ SERVICE (A ____________________ DEMONSTRATION).
10. HE TAUGHT A PERSON HOW TO __________________ IN A ________________________. HE WAS A ________________________ TO THE YOUNG CONVERT WHILE OUT______________________ SOULS. HE WOULD CONTINUE THIS UNTIL ________________ STUDENT LEARNED SUFFICIENTLY, AND THEN THE STUDENT WOULD BECOME A ____________________________.

READ THE NOTES OVER ONE TIME, AND IN TWO WEEKS THE AVERAGE PERSON WILL RETAIN ONLY SIX PERCENT. READ THE NOTES OVER EVERY DAY FOR SIX DAYS, AND THE AVERAGE PERSON WILL RETAIN **62%**.

HOW MANY MINUTES OR HOURS DID YOU STUDY YOUR NOTES AND SOUL-WINNING PRESENTATION EACH DAY ON THIS LESSON? WRITE THE AMOUNT OF DAILY TIME AFTER EACH DAY: ONE POINT FOR EACH MINUTE YOU STUDIED. **15** POINTS FOR EACH DAILY DEVOTION COMPLETED.

Day One___________ Day Two_____________

Day Three__________ Day Four______________

Day Five____________ Day Six______________

TOTAL POINTS _________

NAME__________________________________

Week One
Daily Devotions

Begin the devotions on the first day after the lesson, **Teach Them to Observe (or Do).** Strive to master the main point which is stressed in the devotions. If a person is diligent in learning or mastering each daily devotion it will cause them to experience the abundant life.

Lecture One
Daily Devotions

Day One

Subject: Every Man His Work

SCRIPTURE READING: Mark 13:34-37; II Tim. 1:9; Eph. 2:10; Phil. 2:12

KEY VERSE "...and to every man his work..."Mark 13:34

PRINCIPLE TAUGHT: God saves a person and gives him a definite job or work to perform. We are to work out your own salvation (purpose for which we were saved) with fear and trembling. Every person who is saved has a definite work to do for God.

INDIVIDUAL ACTIVITY: MATCH THE VERSE WITH THE LETTER:

1.____	God has chosen the weak	A. Eph. 2:10
2.____	Work out our own Salvation	B. Phil. 2:12
3.____	According to his own labor	C. II Tim. 1:9
4.____	Saved for a purpose	D. I Cor. 1:27
5.____	Created unto good works	E. 1 Cor. 3:8

FAMILY ACTIVITY: Discuss the different types of service that each member of the family can do. Discuss the specific talent or calling that each member of the family may have.

COMMITMENT PRAYER: Pray that God will direct each member of the family to submit himself to God's will...particularly to witnessing and winning souls.

Day Two
Subject: A Personal Commission to Teach

SCRIPTURE READING: Matt. 28:19-20; II Tim. 2:2; Matt. 10:1-7; Acts 8:26-31.

KEY VERSE II Timothy 2:2, "The same commit thou to faithful men who shall be able to teach others."

PRINCIPLE TAUGHT: Each saved person has a personal commission to teach others. II Timothy 2:2 refutes the false idea... "I'm not a teacher." The Bible teaches that if you are saved you are called to teach others.

INDIVIDUAL ACTIVITY: FILL IN THE BLANKS:

1. "And the things that _______ (Timothy) hast heard of _________ (Paul) among many ___________, the same commit thou to _____________ ________, who shall be able to _______ others also. II Timothy 2:2.

2. "For when for the ___________ ye ought to be _________, ye have need that one _________ you _________..." Hebrews 5:12

FAMILY ACTIVITY: Discuss how well one must learn the Bible before he can teach others. Who should take the lead in teaching his family? Are we exempt from teaching others if some fail to take their responsibility seriously?

COMMITMENT PRAYER: Pray that God will help you to teach others about Jesus and the things of the Bible. Pray that you will become willing to teach others.

Day Three
Subject: Be Ready At All Times

SCRIPTURE READING: II Tim. 2:15; I Pet. 3:15; Acts 17:11;Psalm 1:1-6.

KEY VERSE "Sanctify the Lord God in your hearts and be ready always."I Peter 3:15

PRINCIPLE TAUGHT: The Christian is to master the plan of Salvation so he will be able to give the message of hope to any man at any time.

INDIVIDUAL ACTIVITY: Analyze I Peter 3:15

1. "SANCTIFY" means "set apart", get hold of or master, completely learn.
2. "THE LORD GOD IN YOUR HEARTS" refers to your Salvation.
3. "BE READY ALWAYS", to be ready night or day, be ready in church or in a hostile environment.
4. "TO GIVE EVERY MAN", rich or poor, young or old, black or white.
5. "A REASON OF THE HOPE"; the application of the four spiritual principles of the plan of Salvation.
6. "WITH MEEKNESS AND FEAR", you are not exempt because of your fearful feelings.

FAMILY ACTIVITY: Discuss this verse and ask each member of the family if they are attempting to perform these commands. Discuss how the family can help each other to be obedient.

COMMITMENT PRAYER: "Lord help me to apply myself to learning so I can share thy blessings with others."

Day Four
Subject: Show and Tell

SCRIPTURE READING: Acts 20:20; 18:24-26; 1:1; Luke 11:1

KEY VERSE " ... have shewed you, and have taught you publickly and from house to house."Acts 20:20

PRINCIPLE TAUGHT: Paul's method of making disciples was showing them as well as telling them how to do it. He showed them in public services and then gave them on-the-job training by taking them out and showing them how to win souls by winning souls.

INDIVIDUAL ACTIVITY: Answer the questions.

1. Paul showed and taught ___________. (Acts 20:20)
2. The on-the-job training was called, from ______ to ______. Acts 20:20.
3. Jesus began both ______ ______ and ______. (Acts 1:1).
4. Jesus called the Pharisees hypocrites because they say and _______ ________. (Matthew 23:3).
5. Be ye doers of the Word and not a _________ only...(James 1:22)

FAMILY ACTIVITY: Discuss the Following Saying.

We teach a little by what we say,
We teach more by what we do.
We teach most by what we ARE.

COMMITMENT PRAYER: Pray and ask God to help you teach others by learning the principle of soul-winning so well that you practice it in your daily life. Then show and tell others by giving them on-the-job training.

Day Five
Subject: God's Method Works

SCRIPTURE READING: Acts 19:1-10; 2:41, 42,47; 4:4; 5:14; 6:1, 7.

KEY VERSE: Acts 19:10, "...all they which dwelt in Asia heard the word of the Lord Jesus..."

PRINCIPLE TAUGHT: God's method of training disciples to win souls is to show and tell them publicly, then have one disciple show and tell another disciple from house to house. This method of giving them on-the-job training by taking them out soul-winning, and training them to win souls by winning souls, worked in the New Testament days. It worked so well in Ephesus that twelve disciples (Acts 19:7) under the leadership of Paul and the preachers with him were able to witness to the whole province of Asia in a span of two years.

INDIVIDUAL AND FAMILY ACTIVITY: Match the Quote with the Scripture:

1.____"...added unto them about three thousand souls."
2.____"...Lord added to the church daily..."
3.____"...the number of the man was about five thousand."
4.____"...number of the disciples multiplied..."
5.____ "...the number of the disciples multiplied in Jerusalem greatly..."

A. Acts 2:47
B. Acts 6:7
C. Acts 2:41
D. Acts 4:4
E. Acts 6:1

COMMITMENT PRAYER: Help our Church to stress the New Testament method of training soul-winners. Help me to submit to that training program.

Day Six
Subject: Saved To Train Others

SCRIPTURE READING: Mark 13:34; II Tim. 2:2; Matt. 28: 19-20; Acts 20:20; I Pet. 3:15.

KEY VERSE "Teaching them to observe all things..."Matthew 28:20

PRINCIPLE TAUGHT: Each Christian is personally responsible for winning souls in his daily life. He is to learn to win souls so well that he can train others to win souls by taking them and giving them on-the-job training by winning souls.

INDIVIDUAL ACTIVITY: Match verse with key thought.

1.____	"...every man his work,"	A. Acts 20:20
2.____	A personal commission to teach	B. I Peter 3:15
3.____	"...sanctify the Lord in your hearts..."	C. Mark 13:34
4.____	Show and tell	D. Acts 19:10
5.____	God's method worked in Asia	E. II Tim. 2:2

FAMILY ACTIVITY: Discuss, as a member of your family, how you can help your family develop into better disciples. Who can you personally help train? Can I train some younger member?

COMMITMENT PRAYER: Help us to be doers of the Word instead of hearers of the Word. Help me to follow the example of Jesus who first began to do and to teach.

-Introduction-

Lecture Two

Three Principles Which Make the Difference

Memory Verse

"For I determined not to know any thing among you, save Jesus Christ, and him crucified."
I Corinthians 2:2

Introduction: The three principles which make the difference in soul-winning will enrich the person's ability in every phase of his life.

These valuable truths are taught under the headings of;

The Dumbest Thing You Have Ever Done

Chumming for Fish

Shooing Away Birds

LESSON TWO

THREE PRINCIPLES WHICH MAKE THE DIFFERENCE

INTRODUCTION: There are three Biblical principles God placed in His Word that will help the personal worker have tremendous confidence and success when they are mastered and followed. Remember, these are Biblical principles. Your instructor is not some dynamic salesman who can really "sell the goods." He is a Bible teacher, teaching eternal principles which will enable any serious Christian to perfect himself and become a more consistent, confident soul-winner.

I. THE FIRST PRINCIPLE IS "THE DUMBEST THING YOU HAVE EVER DONE."
   a. REVELATION –This principle is revealed in God's Word in John 3:3, I Cor. 2:14, and I Cor. 2:1-2.
   b. EXPLANATION – In explaining these verses, we will consider each verse separately.
      i. John 3:3 – Jesus told Nicodemus, who was a highly trained leader of the Jews with a master's degree, Except a man be born again, he cannot ---SEE --- the kingdom of God. The word SEE means perceive, understand, or comprehend. The principle taught? The lost man cannot see, comprehend, or understand the kingdom of God or spiritual things.
      ii. I Corinthians 2:14 – "But the natural man..."
         1. The natural man or unsaved in the Bible refers to the unsaved, lost man.

2. The natural man, or unsaved man, has a problem. He can't receive or understand the things of God. "...for they are foolishness unto him: neither can he know [understand] them, because they are spiritually discerned."
    a. The lost man cannot receive them. He cannot know them. Spiritual things are foolishness unto him. He has no spiritual discernment or understanding. He is like an AM radio that has no FM frequency, therefore, he cannot pick up the FM stations. The T.V. picture is fuzzy, and he cannot get a good picture because he has no spiritual antenna.

iii. I Cor. 2:1-2 – In these two verses Paul told the Corinthians that when he came to them while they were still lost, he determined not to know anything but the simple plan of salvation (Jesus Christ and Him crucified). The reason he limited himself in giving the testimony of God to the Corinthians when he came as a personal worker or missionary was because they had no spiritual discernment and could not receive spiritual things (I Cor. 2:14).

c. ILLUSTRATION

i. Imagine that your writer was in a strange city. He went downtown to mail some letters and lost his direction. Because he lost his way he became frustrated. He was late to an appointment and in a hurry. He spotted a nice looking young man who was deaf and mute. Remember the young man could not understand him because of his hearing problem and could not communicate with him because of his speech problem. Your author asks him, "Where is the Post Office?" The young man gave a shrug of the shoulders because he could not understand. Your author, already upset because of the previous difficulties with the deaf mute, began to urge an answer to his question with a louder and louder demand. Finally, he states, "If you don't tell me where the Post Office is, I am going to punch you out!" With that threat , he begins to beat and abuse the young man.

Would you agree that such action would be very foolish and beneath the dignity of an informed, civilized man?

What would happen if I met the same young man the next day? Would he not think, "Here comes that crazy man again," and try to get away from me? At the very least he would be cold towards me and try to avoid me.

d. APPLICATION

i. When a saved person takes the Bible and begins to argue doctrine or discuss scripture with a lost man who cannot "SEE" who cannot receive (understand), and who has no spiritual discernment, only harm can come of it.

ii. Many a well meaning church member literally has taken his Bible and "beat up" and "abused" a poor lost man by arguing "Baptist is better than..." "the King James Version is the ...," "that is a heretical position..."

iii. That is the dumbest thing a child of God can do.

1. It works as an offense to Christ which may cause a lost man to go to hell.
2. Many an interested lost persons who was once friendly and interested now treats Christians, in a cold aloof way. Some ill-informed child of God argued doctrine with them and BEAT THEM UP GOOD!

e. ADMONITION

i. Jesus avoided all questions and stayed on the simple plan of salvation.

ii. Paul said he "DETERMINED" to know only "Jesus Christ and Him crucified" (Simple plan of salvation when he talked to the lost.)

Remember this principle: STATE THE SPIRITUAL PRINCIPLE AND THEN USE A SECULAR EXAMPLE TO ILLUSTRATE THE SPIRITUAL POINT. Avoid arguments, avoid question, stay on the plan of salvation, use illustrations, and the Holy Spirit will do the rest.

II. THE SECOND PRINCIPLE IS CHUMMING FOR FISH

a. REVELATION

i. This principle is revealed in Matthew 4:19, "...Follow me and I will make you fishers of men," and in Luke 5:10, "...henceforth thou shalt catch men." Jesus stated the same principle in a different way when He commanded, "...be wise **as** a serpent and **as** harmless **as** a doves."

b. EXPLANATION

   i. There must be a correlation between fishing for fish and fishing for men.
   ii. The term, chumming for fish, came from the practice of fishermen throwing bait into the water in order to attract schools of fish. After chumming or throwing out bait, the fishermen found they could catch the fish much easier.
   iii. These verses teach that there is a scriptural way to approach people so they will be more likely to listen to the gospel and be saved.
   iv. Chumming for fish also teaches a planned method of approaching people: "I will make you fishers of men"...you will catch men.

c. APPLICATION

There are two truths, when joined together, produce the principle which aids in catching men.

   i. When a fisherman goes fishing, he doesn't use bait he likes. He may love strawberry shortcake and ice cream, but that old fish is attracted to a worm. The fishes' favorite dessert may be a smelly sardine.
   ii. When a ship runs into difficulty on the high seas, it sends a distress signal of "S O S"

iii. When the soul-winner goes witnessing, he does not use bait he likes, but he uses bait the PROSPECT LIKES.

iv. When the personal worker goes into a home, he may feel some doubt, fear or nervousness. He may have some spiritual fear of "DISTRESS." WHEN ONE HAS DISTRESS, THINK SOS." "SOS" stands for three areas of conversation in which the prospect like to talk:

1. S. – The letter "S" stands for self-interest (prospects self-interest).
    a. He likes to talk about his family, hobbies, vacations, etc.
2. O. – The letter "O" stands for occupation.
    a. The average person likes to brag or gripe about his job.
    b. Remember, being a homemaker or going to school are two difficult jobs.
3. S. – The final "S" stands for spiritual background or soul-winning message.

d. ADMONITION

i. We are to follow Jesus and go fishing.

1. The visitation team goes to a home armed with the knowledge that when one goes fishing for men, he uses bait the prospect likes. With his new outline of SOS he begins to ask questions which will keep the prospect talking about his own interests. The team simply uses

their God-given tools (eyes, ears, personality, mouth) to keep the prospect talking about his interest as they guide him to a place where they can share the facts of God's love and provision with the sinner.

ii. WE are to help the fish (chum) to be attracted to the gospel. We spend 10-20 minutes asking questions about what the prospect like to talk about. As we talk, we know he will enjoy our conversation because he is doing most of the talking while we direct the conversation toward the plan of salvation. The distress is gone because of the planned SOS

iii. We then make the transition from a social visit with a purpose to the soul-winning effort by ASKING five simple approach questions:

    1. I can see you are interested in spiritual things, aren't you?
    2. Let me ask you, have you ever considered your need for eternal life?
    3. If you should die today, do you KNOW FOR SURE that you would go to heaven?
    4. You would like to know wouldn't you"? (nodding your head in the affirmative)
    5. If I could take your Bible and show you how you could know for sure, would you consider doing what the Bible says?

iv. The soul-winner can proceed with confidence because he has permission from the prospect.

III. THE THIRD PRINCIPLE IS "SHOOING AWAY BIRDS"

a. REVELATION

i. The principle of "shooing away birds" is taught in the parable of the sower in Matthew 13:3-8, 18-23, and in Ephesians 6:16.

b. EXPLANATION

i. In the parable of the sower, the sower sows "seed," and there are four different end results to the seeds. The one reaction which teaches the need to learn to shoo away birds is the first reaction of the seed falling by the wayside.

ii. The sower went, the seed fell, the birds ate it up.

iii. The interpretation of these three symbols are:

1. The sower is someone (soul-winner) going with the seed.
2. The seed is the Word of God or the message (Matthew 15:19).
3. The birds represents the devil (verse 19).

iv. In Ephesians 6:16 the Christian soldier is commanded to take the shield of faith in order to quench all the "fiery darts" (arrows) of the wicked (wicked one or the devil). The devil has access to a person's mind and shoots all types of thoughts into people's minds.

v. One needs to know how to shoo away these birds. If the devil is going to try to steal away the message when one gives the plan of salvation, then one needs to know how to shoo away these birds. If the devil is going to shoot thoughts into the person's mind while you are witnessing, then one needs to learn how to prevent him from doing so.

c. APPLICATION

The question arises, "How can I learn to shoo away birds and keep down any questions which may hinder my visit?" One can shoo away birds by practicing five principles.

i. Use the conversational dialogue instead of monologue while witnessing to him.
ii. Ask the prospect questions while witnessing to him.
iii. Call the prospect by name while witnessing to him.
iv. Use gestures which will keep the prospect's attention focused-in on what you are saying to him.
v. Use eye contact while witnessing to him.

d. ADMONITION

One goes witnessing with the knowledge that the devil will attack. Armed with the knowledge and with the knowledge of how to OFFSET this attack, the soul-winner gains great confidence and will increase his effectiveness in witnessing. He will see more genuine conversions. He will catch more fish!

SUMMARY: NOTE SOME OF THE THINGS YOU HAVE LEARNED:

1. The lost man cannot understand spiritual things, so it is "DUMB" to discuss doctrine or answer questions.

2. The soul-winner concentrates on giving the plan of salvation which is contained in four spiritual principles (scriptures).
3. One uses physical illustrations that the prospect can understand in order to illustrate the spiritual principles. The Holy Spirit illuminates the sinner's mind and convicts him of sin.

NOTE: Since you are the first person who is following the principle of illustration and the sinner is (for the first time) really understanding, he will appreciate your visit and will respond in a friendly way.

4. When a person armed with the knowledge of the principle of chumming for fish talks in the sinner's areas of interest as he guides the prospect toward the soul-winning message, it creates a receptive mood and removes DISTRESS.
5. When the soul-winner goes through the five approach questions and gets permission to witness to the prospect, it gives added confidence.
6. When a person knows how the devil will attack as he gives the soul-winning message, it gives added confidence.
7. When the soul-winner knows how to shoo away birds and prevent damage to his visits, it gives great confidence.

MASTER THESE PRINCIPLES, AND IT WILL MAKE A GREAT DIFFERENCE IN YOUR WITNESSING AND CATCHING MEN FOR JESUS!

Three Principles Which Make The Difference Lecture Two

1. The natural _______ cannot _______, understand, or perceive ______________ things.
2. Jesus first established the ____________ principle and then illustrated it by using some __________________ (______________) which the sinner understood.
3. Paul determined not to ________ anything except Jesus Christ and Him ______________ (simple plan of salvation) while talking to ________ men.
4. Many a well-intended __________ member has taken his _________ and "beat up" and "abused" a poor lost man, thus committing the ____________ act that he ever committed.
5. There must be a correlation or ____________ between fishing for ________ and fishing for _______.
6. S O S. stands for three areas of ________________ in which the prospect likes to __________.
7. Generally we spend 10 to 20 ___________ asking ______________ which keeps the prospect ___________ about things in which he is interested.
8. We then make the ______________ of a social visit with a purpose to the ______ ____________ effort by asking five approach ______________.
9. The principle of shooing ________ _________ is taught in the parable of the ____________.
10. The sower is ___________ (soul-winner) going with the _________. The seed is the ________ of God or the ___________, the _________ represent the _________.

11. Master these _____________, and it will make a _________ difference in your ____________ and _________ men for Jesus.

READ THE NOTES OVER ONE TIME, AND IN TWO WEEKS THE AVERAGE PERSON WILL RETAIN ONLY SIX PERCENT. READ THE NOTES OVER EVERY DAY FOR SIX DAYS, AND THE AVERAGE PERSON WILL RETAIN **62%**.

HOW MANY MINUTES OR HOURS DID YOU STUDY YOUR NOTES AND SOUL-WINNING PRESENTATION EACH DAY ON THIS LESSON? WRITE THE AMOUNT OF DAILY TIME AFTER EACH DAY: ONE POINT FOR EACH MINUTE YOU STUDIED; 15 POINTS FOR EACH DAILY DEVOTION COMPLETED.

Day One___________ Day Two_____________

Day Three__________ Day Four______________

Day Five____________ Day Six______________

TOTAL POINTS _________

NAME__________________________________

Week Two
Daily Devotions

Begin the devotions the next day after the seminar. Give yourself 15 points for each day you do your devotion.
Each Daily Devotion is very important and reinforces the principles taught in the seminar.

Lecture Two

Daily Devotions

Day One

Subject: After His Kind

SCRIPTURE READING: Genesis 1:11-12; 1:20-28; 8:17; Luke 13:6-9

KEY VERSE: Genesis 1:11, "...the herb yielding seed, and the fruit tree yielding fruit after his Kind,..."

PRINCIPLE TAUGHT: God created everything to be fruitful. The law of God is for every living thing to reproduce itself by bearing substance just like itself. After establishing the principle he looked and said it was good. The evolutionist cannot find the missing link because there is no missing LINK. The whole chain is missing! Every healthy species is to glorify its maker by reproducing itself. The principle is true from the lowest form of life to the highest MAN!

INDIVIDUAL ACTIVITY: Things God Made:

1.__	Let there be _____.	A. Gen. 1:20
2.__	God called the dry land ______.	B. Gen. 1:3
3.__	And ______ that may fly above.	C. Gen. 126
4.__	Let us make ______ in our image.	D. Gen. 1:10
5.__	God saw ______ that He had made.	E. Gen. 1:31

FAMILY ACTIVITY: Discuss which takes greater faith to believe, evolution or the Genesis account of creation. Discuss the principle that everything is to reproduce "after his kind."

Day Two
Subject: Children Are an Heritage of the LORD

SCRIPTURE READING: Gen. 1:28; I Sam. 1:11-19; Job1:1-5; Eph. 6:4.

KEY VERSE: Psalm 127:3, "Lo, children are an heritage of the LORD."

PRINCIPLE TAUGHT: The Bible teaches that God created man and commanded him to be fruitful or have a family. The Bible teaches that God gives children and they should be raised for the honor and glory of God. If the parents will raise their children by the Bible, then they will be a credit to their parents and bring glory to God.

INDIVIDUAL ACTIVITY: Answer the Questions.

1. Fathers are to raise their children in the ____________ and __________________ of the ______________. Eph. 6:4.

2. Children are an heritage of the ______ and the fruit of the womb is ______ _______ Ps. 127:3

3. When did Job pray and make special offerings to God for his children? ________________ Job 1:5

FAMILY ACTIVITY: Discuss: When a young man and a young woman are married, does he have to be a Mr. Atlas and she a Miss America before they can have children?

COMMITMENT PRAYER: Lord, help me to fit into my family and have a proper attitude.

Day Three
Subject: Fruit of the Holy Spirit

SCRIPTURE READING: Gal. 5:22-24, 25-26; Eph. 5:18-20; John 16:13-15; Rom. 8:26-27.

KEY VERSE: Galatians 5:22-23, "...the fruit of the Spirit is love, joy, peace, longsuffering, gentleness, goodness, faith..."

PRINCIPLE TAUGHT: The Bible teaches that the Holy Spirit was sent to aid the believer in living a successful Christian life. The fruit of the Holy Spirit is clearly listed in Galatians 5:22-23. This is the fruit of the Holy Spirit in the life of a believer. It is not the fruit of believers.

INDIVIDUAL ACTIVITY: Match the Verses with Statement:

1. __ The Holy Spirit aids the believer in prayer	A. John 16:13
2.__ Be filled with the Spirit	B. Rom. 8:26-27
3.__ The fruit of the Spirit is	C. Gal. 5:22-23
4.__ He will not speak of Himself	D. Acts 10:38
5.__ Jesus was anointed with the Holy Ghost	E. Eph. 5:18

FAMILY ACTIVITY: Discuss the meaning of the fruit of the Spirit in Gal. 5:22. Are these different fruits dominating my life?

COMMITMENT PRAYER: Oh, God, help me submit to you and to Thy Word so the fruit of the Spirit will be manifest in my life.

Day Four
Subject: The Fruit of the Saved

SCRIPTURE READING: John 15:8, 16; Prov. 11:30;Rev. 4:11; I Cor. 10:31.

KEY VERSE: "The Fruit of the righteous [saved] is a tree of life;..." Proverbs 11:30

PRINCIPLE TAUGHT: The saved are to bear fruit for the Lord just as all living beings are to bear fruit. The fruit of the righteous, or saved, is winning souls. The fruit of an apple tree is apples, not leaves. The test of a good milk cow is how much milk she gives and the butterfat content, not the contented look she may have. John 15:8 states that one who is declared to be a disciple glorifies God when he bears fruit or wins souls.

INDIVIDUAL AND FAMILY ACTIVITY: Analyze & Discuss John 15:16.

1. I HAVE CHOSEN: elected or saved.
2. AND ORDAINED: appointed or set you to it.
3. THAT YOU SHOULD GO: the saved are chosen to go.
4. AND BRING FORTH FRUIT: He is talking to disciples (not the Holy Spirit). Fruit of the saved is winning souls.
5. FRUIT SHOULD REMAIN: This means God has a way to developing new converts so they too can become fruitful.
6. ASK ANYTHING: If a believer will (1) go, (2) win souls, and (3) take care of the new converts, he can ask God to do the impossible and He will do it.

COMMITMENT PRAYER: Lord, if I was designed to be fruitful (win souls), help me to submit to you, learn to witness, and become a soul-winner

Day Five
Subject: The Simple Process of Harvesting

SCRIPTURE READING: Psalms 126:6

KEY VERSE: "He that goeth forth and weepeth bearing precious seed..."Psalms 126:6

PRINCIPLE TAUGHT: God outlines the simple step of harvesting lost souls in Psalm 126:6. He promises (doubtless) a sure harvest if one will GO, WEEP (be concerned), and SOW the Seed (Word of God). This is the same principle of harvesting as in the physical realm. One must sow, water and reap. The soul-winner must sow, water (weep), and he will doubtless come again with REJOICING, bringing in the sheaves (souls).

INDIVIDUAL ACTIVITY: Fill in the Blanks.

1. "...I am made all things to all *men* that I might by all means ________ some." I Corinthians 9:22.
2. "For the Son of man is come to seek and to _________ that which was lost." Luke 19:10.
3. "...go out into the highways and hedges, and ____________ *them* to come in, that my house may be filled." Luke 14:23.

FAMILY ACTIVITY: Discuss: What friends and acquaintances may our family be able to reach for Christ? What would be a good approach to take?

COMMITMENT PRAYER: Lord, help us have your leadership in approaching our lost friends and family.

Day Six
Subject: Glorifying Christ

SCRIPTURE READING: John 15:8, 16; Gen 1:24; Prov. 11:30

KEY VERSE: "Herein is my Father glorified, that ye bear much fruit;..."John 15:8

PRINCIPLE TAUGHT: Every healthy, living creature which God created is to be fruitful. This is true in the spiritual realm as well as in all other realms. Every healthy child of God is to reproduce himself and glorify his God by personally winning souls. The fruit of the saved is winning another to Jesus. God is more pleased with fruitless apple trees in a fruitful apple orchard than He is with a fruitless child of God in a soul-winning Church. Both are displeasing to God.

INDIVIDUAL ACTIVITY: Match Subject with Scripture:

1.___ After his kind	A. Gal. 5:22
2.___ Children are an heritage	B. Gen. 1:25
3.___ Fruit of the Spirit	C. Ps. 126:6
4.___ Fruit of the saved	D. Ps. 127:3
5.___ A simple process of harvesting	E. Prov. 11:30

FAMILY ACTIVITY: Discuss the Four Spiritual Laws.

COMMITMENT PRAYER: Lord, help each of us to help each other to master the art of harvesting lost souls so we can better glorify you.

-Introduction-

Lecture Three

How to Have a Successful Visit Every Time

Memory Verse

"They that sow in tears shall reap in joy. He that goeth forth and weepeth, bearing precious seed, shall doubtless come again with rejoicing, bringing his sheaves *with him*."
Psalm 126:5-6

Introduction: There are five possible visits that a soul-winning team may encounter. This lesson will show how to have a successful visit every time.

They win someone to the Lord.

They witness effectively, but the person is not saved.

They visit the sick or shut-in.

They receive a hostile reception.

They do not find anyone at home.

Lecture Three

How to Have a Successful Visit Every Time

Introduction: The above statement, at first glance, would appear to be a statement made by a fool or a trick subject made to attract one's attention. It is not a trick on the part of the writer, but a honest attempt to make the reader accept the Bible literally the and show him how to have a successful visit every time.

There are five types of soul-winning visits:

1. The soul-winner witnesses and the sinner receives the Lord as his Saviour.
2. The soul-winner witnesses and the sinner does not receive the Lord as his Saviour.
3. The soul-winner goes to the sick or shut-in and witnesses for the Lord.
4. The soul-winner goes but is received with hostility.
5. The soul-winner goes and goes and goes and does not find anyone home.

I. The soul-winner witnesses and the sinner receives the Lord
   a. Everyone acclaims this as a successful visit.
      i. A sinner is saved from hell.
      ii. The soul-winner has a soul-winner's joy (Psa. 126:5-6)
      iii. The inhabitants of heaven rejoice. (Luke 15:7-10)

    iv. The heart of God is made glad.

II. The soul-winner witnesses and the sinner does not receive the lord

  a. Many soul-winner teams come back in dejection.
    i. They act like a puppy who has been scolded.
    ii. Their reaction is due to their walking by sight or depending upon feeling instead of walking by faith.
  b. Many people have a deliberate disposition.
    i. They never make any decision on the spot.
    ii. They fully consider every decision carefully before making commitment. When they make a commitment, they become the most solid members in the church.
  c. A successful visit is made.
    i. When a person goes in the right spirit.
    ii. When he humbly gives the soul-winning message.
    iii. When he followed God's designed plan for a sure harvest: One sows, another waters, but God gives the increase. (I Corinthians 3:5-7)
    iv. If you do not classify it as a successful visit, then the pastor who does not have people saved every sermon is a failure too.
    v. When many sow. Much watering and years later in a hospital room someone else reaps. When a person walks by faith and gives the plan of salvation, he is following God's plan for a sure harvest and we must count the visit a success.

III. The soul-winner visits the sick or shut-ins.

  a. A very poor spirit

   i. Some staff members, when assigned to make hospital or shut-in visits, react as if placed on K.P. duty.
   ii. Many church members are permanently wounded when they are not visited in the hospital by their fellow church members. Often no one comes except one of the paid staff or the pastor. They never get over the disappointment because they think no one really cares.

b. The visit is appreciated most
   i. By someone who is sick, perhaps facing surgery and an uncertain future.
   ii. By the most lonely, neglected people in the world who are in the welfare wards or convalescence homes.

c. The most effective time to visit
   i. When they are facing death or an uncertain future (right before surgery).
   ii. When they are cast aside, left to die, and abandoned by their family, friends, and the world in an old folk's home.

d. A successful visit
   i. "...I was sick, and ye visited me... when saw we thee sick, or in prison, and came unto thee? And the King shall answer and say unto them, Verily I say unto you, Inasmuch as ye have done *it* unto one of the least of these my brethren, ye have done *it* unto me." (Matthew 25:26-40)
   ii. If Jesus is going to remember the visit and account it as a visit unto Himself, then you should count it as a successful visit.

IV. The soul-winner goes and is received with hostility.

a. Some create their own rejection

i. When one makes a stiff, unnatural approach, he creates uncertainty and rejection in the one he is visiting.

ii. When he has a sickly, fake grin, he makes the prospect suspicious by his put-on friendliness.

iii. They create their own problem by acting like a weirdo.

b. Some deserve their rejection.

i. There are two crews in most churches: a building crew and a wrecking crew. One crew is getting them in while another crew is running them off.

ii. It could be said the only mistake the sinner makes in slamming the door in the so-called soul-winner's face is that he slams the door too soon. He should have waited until he could have slammed the door on his neck instead of in front of his face.

iii. Some sinners should be rewarded for their hostility instead of rebuked. Some so-called soul-winners are so rude and ignorant in their approach.

c. Some sinners have been wounded by so-called Christians

i. Many have been hurt by people who claim to be a Christian and are hostile toward all Christians, and rightly so.

ii. A young man had been robbed of his mother and has lived with this rejection because some so-called preacher ran off with his mother when he was a little boy.

iii. Some have grown up in poverty and lived with a broken-spirited father who was fleeced by a so-called "Christian businessman."

iv. Some have never understood why things were never like they used to be. They have had to give up relatives and friends because of an "old-fashioned church split."

d. We are to love the wounded too.

i. Their problem is not with us (we haven't offended them); so don't take their insults personally.

ii. You are not better than your master who was verbally attacked.

iii. Roll with the punches. Love them anyway. Demonstrate the Christian attitude.

iv. Later, befriend them. Find some way to compliment them and take a long-range approach in overcoming their hostility.

v. Never be a baby and cry about someone slamming a door in your face.

vi. We are to show the love of Christ to all creatures, which includes the hostile also.

e. A successful visit

i. Matthew 5:11-12 "Blessed are ye, when men shall revile you, and persecute *you*, and shall say all manner of evil against you falsely, for my sake. Rejoice, and be exceeding glad: for great *is* your reward in heaven..."

    ii. If Christ promises you a reward for encountering hostility, then you had better count the visit as a successful visit, and rejoice.

V. The soul-winner goes and no one is home

a. Eight not at home visits
    i. At first sight, a person would react: "A person would have to be a fool to think he could make a successful visit out of eight not-at-home calls.
    ii. There is no way to make eight not-at-home visits a successful visit unless we go back to the Bible method of training soul-winners

b. The wrong method of soul-winning
    i. It is evident that the average church has not discovered God's method in soul-winning when one observes:
        1. The confusion which prevails during the visitation services – assigning of cards, visitation teams, the disorder and disorganization, which prevails before, during and after the visitation service.
        2. The small number of people saved as a result of the visitation service.
        3. The constant effort of the pastor or out-reach director to enlist, keep, motivate and direct the out-reach ministry of the church.

c. The Bible method of soul-winning
    i. The soul-winning team consists of two people
        1. A soul-winner trainer
        2. A silent partner trainee
    ii. Paul's method of training:

1. He would show them publicly (soul-winning demonstrations – Acts 20:20)
2. He would teach them publicly by going over each point and then demonstrating it.
3. He would become the teacher-example from house to house.
4. He would give them on-the-job training by taking the silent partner-trainee out into the homes, showing him and teaching him until he was trained enough to become the soul-winner trainer himself. Then Paul would begin the process all over again with a new silent partner-trainee.

iii. Paul's method of training soul-winners is God's method
   1. An older, more mature Christian who has been trained serves as the soul-winner trainer.
   2. The pastor know how many soul-winner trainers he has, so he prepares the visitation packets for them in advance of the visitation service.
   3. The soul-winner trainer is over the silent partner-trainee. He is to teach the silent partner trainee how to win souls over a given period of time while they are out witnessing as a team.
   4. The trainer takes the trainee into his car. The visit begins by the trainer recounting the procedure and dialogue of the soul-winning plan to and with his trainee. They

come to the first house, but no one is home. They leave the visitation folder with a short, personal note and leave. The soul-winner training resumes. They come to the next house. No one is home. They repeat the same procedure each time the training continues. The vital areas of the soul-wining plan and procedure are mastered. Note the areas covered

a. They leave the visitation service
b. They go over the five approach questions
c. The four spiritual principles and how to illustrate them are studied.
d. The proper way to close is discussed.
e. The prayer is said in closing.

d. A successful visit
   i. They leave the visitation service.
   ii. The soul-winner trainer begins to teach the silent partner trainee
   iii. They come to the first house. No one is at home so they leave a note.
   iv. They continue the training session as they go to the next house.
      1. Recently a young ministerial student, with tears in his eyes, told me after spending all afternoon in calling and finding no one at home, "Sir, I feel like I have been in the greatest Bible college classroom I have ever attended this afternoon. You'll never know

how much your instruction has meant to me."

2. I received a long distance telephone call from a young man who was so excited he could hardly talk. He said, "I know why no one was home when you and I went calling two weeks ago. I needed the instruction which you gave me during the visit to lead the man I won to the Lord tonight. Without it, I would have sent him to hell. What you taught me that night saved the visit, and the man is going to be baptized Sunday."

v. If you go out and impart eternal truth to a younger Christian, walk by faith, manifest the proper attitude in front of him, and help develop him in witnessing, shouldn't you call that a successful visit?

A Two Edged Sword

One simple act can encourage at least two people. If a person accepts the role of being a trainer there are two possible encouragements which may occur. The gratification of being the trainer as he sees the week by week improvement of his trainee. He assumes the role of a proud parent who guides his son through a challenging task.

The trainee feels good about himself as he studies, receives encouragement from his trainer and grows his ability to win souls. A lifetime bond is formed as the two learn to be an effective team in obeying the Lord in winning souls. Add to this to the joy of winning souls and the blessing they receive from the Holy Spirit, and they will keep soul-winning.

We have shown that in the greatest work on earth, God has a method of developing new workers. This classroom showing and teaching and then showing the new worker how to perfect himself by giving on-the-job training has the potential of rapid growth.

Therefore, we can expect the Devil to make his greatest counterattack in order to stop this growth. One of his greatest methods is **discouragement**.

It is very easy to see how this method of defeating a person would be very successful and cause the worker to become discouraged and quit.

House after house after house with no one home. Then when you finally get someone saved and are exuberant with joy, that joy is turned to **disappointment** when the person does not keep his promise and come to church. Especially if this happens many times (see section 8, discouragement, in how to defeat the devil for further explanation).

We are not out visiting people in their homes because it is good spiritual exercise. We do it because it is mandated of the Lord. People are condemned and going to Hell and must be rescued. Visiting people in their homes does not make a **person a better Christian**, but it does make a person an OBEDIENT CHRISTIAN. We are commanded to go to every creature. In order to do so we must literally go or walk by faith. **Success or failure will not alter** this command. If **we obey and go we can have a successful visit every time**

"How To Have A Successful Visit Every Time"

Lecture III

1. The soul-winner witnesses, and the sinner ______________ the Lord. Everyone acclaims this as a ______________ visit.
2. Many soul-winners come back in ______________ like a puppy who has been ______________.
3. He followed God's designed ______________ of "one __________, another ______________, but God gives the ________________ (I Corinthians 3:5-7)
4. Many church members are permanently ____________ when they are not visited in the ________________ by their fellow church members.
5. The visit is appreciated the ______________ by someone who is sick, perhaps facing ___________ and uncertain _________________.
6. Some soul-winners create their own ______________. They make the prospect suspicious by their put-on ___________.
7. We are to __________________ the wounded too. Their problem is not with ______________. We haven't offended them. So don't take their ________________ personally.
8. "_____________ are ye, when *men* shall ____________ you, and __________ *you*, and shall say all manner of evil against you falsely, for my ___________. Rejoice and be exceeding ____________: for great *is* your _____________ in heaven:... (Matthew 5:11-12)

9. There is no way to make eight not-at-home visits a ____________ visit unless we go back to the Bible ___________ of training ___________________.
10. The Apostle Paul will show them publicly _______________ demonstration (Acts 20:20) and he would _________________ publicly.
11. He would become the teacher-example from _______________ to ________________. He would give them on-the-job _________________ by taking the silent-partner trainee out into the home _______________ him, teaching him until he learned enough to become the ____________________ himself.

Read the notes over one time, and in two weeks the average person will retain only six percent. Read the notes over every day for six days, and the average person will retain sixty-two percent.

How many minutes or hours did you study your notes and soul-winning presentation each day on this lesson? Write the amount of daily time after each day.

Day One___________ Day Two_____________

Day Three__________ Day Four______________

Day Five____________ Day Six______________

Week Three
Daily Devotions

Begin the first devotion of this week the day following the seminar. Remember each Daily Devotion is designed to reinforce the principles taught in the seminar. Give yourself 15 points for each Daily Devotion completed.

Lecture Three
Day One
Subject: Making Heaven Rejoice

SCRIPTURE READING: Luke 15:1-24; Hebrews 12:2

KEY VERSE: Luke 15:7, "...joy shall be in heaven over one sinner that repenteth..."

PRINCIPLE TAUGHT: The one parable of Luke 15 (THIS parable, not these parables) has to do with seeking and saving sinners. In verse seven and ten, Jesus said that there is rejoicing in heaven over one sinner being saved. The old father represents God the Father, who was the happiest person of all when the wayward child came home. When one causes all of heaven, especially God the Father, to rejoice by winning souls then he will experience the joy of the Victorious, Abundant Life.

INDIVIDUAL ACTIVITY: Fill in the Blanks:

They that sow in _______ shall reap in _______. He that ________ forth and __________, bearing precious seed, shall doubtless come again with _________ bringing his sheaves *with him*. (Psalm 126:5-6)

FAMILY ACTIVITY: Discuss: Is a soul that was worth Jesus dying for worth crying for? How long has it been since you wept over a lost soul?

COMMITMENT PRAYER: Lord, help me imitate Jesus by learning to weep over lost souls.

Day Two
Subject: Sowing and Watering

SCRIPTURE READING: Matt. 13:3-8,18-23; Eccl. 11:4; I Cor. 3:5-8; John 4:35-38

KEY VERSE: "I have planted, Apollos watered; but God gave the increase."I Cor. 3:6

PRINCIPLE TAUGHT: The soul-winner should earnestly present the soul-winning message to the lost. After he has presented the message of Salvation he should realize God's method of soul-winning is for one to sow, another to water and for God to give the increase. If a person follows God's method in soul-winning (sowing and watering) he should not depend on results before being happy. He should depend upon God's promises and follow God's procedure of sowing and watering with full assurance of reaping.

INDIVIDUAL ACTIVITY: Match Subject with Scripture:

1. First, pray for the sinner	A. Ps. 126:6
2. Second, go out and sow the Seed	B. Luke 10:2
3. Third, others pray and witness	C. Matt. 13:3
4. Fourth, don't give up	D. Gal. 6:9
5. Fifth, come again rejoicing...	E. I Cor. 3:6

FAMILY ACTIVITY: Make a list of those to whom you should witness (sowing). Make a list of those for whom you should continue to pray as you continue your witnessing (watering).COMMITMENT PRAYER: Lord, help me continue with full assurance of sowing and watering until our loved ones and friends are all saved.

Day Three
Subject: Visiting Jesus

SCRIPTURE READING: Matt. 25:34-40; Acts 9:1-5

KEY VERSE: Matthew 25:40, "...as ye have done *it* unto one of the least of these my breathren, ye have done *it* unto me."

PRINCIPLE TAUGHT: When one visits the sick and shut-in's, Jesus accounts the visit as a visit unto Himself and will remember it and reward the one who makes the visit.

INDIVIDUAL ACTIVITY: Match Statement with Scripture:

1.___	To visit the fatherless and widows.	A. Mark 2:17
2.___	Ye have done it unto me.	B. Matt. 25:40
3.___	They that are whole need not a physician.	C. II Cor. 12:9
4.___	The prayer of faith shall save the sick.	D. James 1:27
5.___	My strength is made perfect in weakness	E. James 5:15

FAMILY ACTIVITY: Make a list of the sick shut-in's of the church and your immediate neighborhood who would appreciate a visit from you.

COMMITMENT PRAYER: Lord, help me to have a tender heart toward the sick and unfortunate. Help me consider your will toward them and do it.

Day Four
Subject: Candidates for Reward

SCRIPTURE READING: Matt. 5:11-13; I Pet. 1:6-9; II Tim. 3:12; II Cor. 4:17-18

KEY VERSE: Matthew 5:12, "... for great *is* your reward **in heaven**..."

PRINCIPLE TAUGHT: When one goes out and has a poor reception from the person he is witnessing to or has a door slammed in his face, he should rejoice instead of accepting the rebuff personally. The sinner's problem is not the soul-winner. The soul-winner has not offended or wronged him. The sinner's problem is with himself or with God. If the Christian witnesses, regardless of the reception, he should be content because he has been obedient to God and God will reward him for it.

INDIVIDUAL ACTIVITY: Match Crowns with Scripture:

1.___ Crown of Incorruption	A. I Pet. 5:4
2.___ Crown of Rejoicing	B. I Thess. 2:19
3.___ Crown of Life	C. II Tim. 4:8
4.___ Crown of Glory	D. Rev. 2:10
5.___ Crown of Righteousness	E. I Cor. 9:25

FAMILY ACTIVITY: Discuss the subject: Who will be the superstars of Heaven? The superstars of sports and of the business world today are those who turn away from the world in order to win souls.

COMMITMENT PRAYER: Lord, help me to endure the tribulation and insults of the world in order to please you and win souls.

Day Five
Subject: Walking by Faith

SCRIPTURE READING: Hebrews 4:11-12; 10:38; 11:1-6 Acts 20:20

KEY VERSE: Hebrews 10:38, "...the just [saved] shall live by faith..."

PRINCIPLE TAUGHT: God's method of training is for a soul-winner to take a silent partner-trainee out soul-winning and teach him how to wins souls by showing and teaching him (on-the-job training) how to do it by doing it. If one takes another and teaches him by giving him on-the-job training, he will have a successful visit even though he does not find anyone at home. He walks by faith, imparts eternal truth and follows the New Testament pattern of training another to win souls. Thus he has a successful visit.

INDIVIDUAL ACTIVITY: Name the Men of Faith

1. By faith _______ offered a more excellent sacrifice. Heb. 11:4
2. Who was strong in faith? ________ Rom. 4:16-20
3. He built an Ark by faith. ________ Heb. 11:7
4./ faith refused wealth. ________ Heb. 11:24-26
5. We are to _______ the faith of the Pastor Heb. 13:7

FAMILY ACTIVITY: Discuss: How can a family walk by faith today?

COMMITMENT PRAYER: Lord, help us to grow in faith and knowledge so we can please you.

Day Six
Subject: A Winner Every Time

SCRIPTURE READING: Luke 15:10; I Cor. 3:8; Matt. 5:11-12; 25:40; Heb. 10:38; Acts 20:20; Ps. 126:5-6

KEY VERSE: Psalm 126:6, "... shall doubtless come again rejoicing..."

PRINCIPLE TAUGHT: If one goes out and wins someone he has a successful visit. If one goes out and follows God's pattern of sowing or watering he has a successful visit. If one visits the sick and Jesus accounts the visit as one to Himself then the soul-winner has a successful visit. If one goes out in the name and spirit of Christ but is received with hostility he has a successful visit because he will be rewarded for his effort. If one goes and goes and goes but finds no one at home, his visit must be counted as a success if he follows God's method of soul-winning training and uses the time to train another. Therefore the principle taught...in soul-winning visitations, a person is a winner every time.

INDIVIDUAL ACTIVITY: Match the meaning with the verse

1.	_____ One sows, another waters	A. I Cor. 3:8
2.	_____There is rejoicing in Heaven	B. Matt25:40
3.	_____Ye did it unto me	C. Matt 5:11-12
4.	_____Rejoice and be exceeding glad	D. Acts 20:20
5.	_____Showed and taught	E. Luke 15:7

FAMILY ACTIVITY: Discuss the five types of visits given above.

-Introduction-

Lecture Four

Beating the Devil at His Own Game.

Memory Verse

"Be sober, be vigilant; because your adversary the devil, as a roaring lion, walketh about, seeking whom he may devour:" I Peter 5:8

Introduction: When a person begins to give a soul-wining talk the Devil instantly attempts to destroy the visit.

There are seven particular places that he will attack. In this lesson the personal worker is given information which will offset and control these attacks.

The particular places he will attack are;

1. The point at the **Davenport (sofa)**
2. The point at the **Door**
3. The point of **Dialogue**
4. The point of **Decision**
5. The point of **Distraction**
6. The point of **Duplication**
7. The point of **Distortion**
8. The point of **Discouragement**

Lecture Four
"Beating The Devil At His Own Game"
(...your adversary the devil..." –I Peter 5:8)

Introduction: The soul-winner should be constantly aware of his adversary, the devil. He is always on the job. When the seed (Word) is sown, the bird (devil) is there to steal it (Matt 13). He should heed the admonition. "Be sober, be vigilant;..." Why? "...because your adversary the devil, as a roaring lion, walketh about seeking whom he may devour:"

The devil was...

1. Strong enough to blind, bind, and overpower the strongest man who ever lived (Samson).
2. Wise enough to out-fox, out-maneuver and check-mate the wisest man who ever lived (Solomon). He put him on his deathbed with the knowledge that his life's work and kingdom was destroyed.
3. Subtle enough to catch the man after God's own heart off guard, lure him into sin, and wound him (David).
4. Able to sift the chief Apostle into denying his Lord, warm himself by the enemy's fire, and openly curse Him (Peter).

"Be sober, be vigilant;..." Watch your adversary. He is dangerous, but be of good cheer! Greater is He (Holy Spirit) who is within you than he who is without (1 Jn. 4:4b). Stay within the hedge (Will Of God) as Job did, and harm the devil causes will be turned into victories by the grace of God.

God promised Paul, I will keep you from those to whom now I send you (Acts 26:17).

I. The Wiles of the Devil – "Put on the whole armour of God, that ye may be able to stand against the wiles of the devil." (Eph 6:11)

A. Wiles means methods. (lie in wait)
   1. If the devil has methods, then one can discover what they are.
   2. The F.B.I. discovers the methods or habits or similarities of the crimes, which leads to the capture of the criminal.

B. Wiles are deceptive.
   1. He is the terrifying terror – "...roaring lion..." (1 Pet. 5:8).
   2. He shoots tormenting torches into one's mind – "...fiery darts of the wicked [one]." (Eph 6:16).
   3. He is the town tough (James 4:7).
   4. He builds towering towers – "...strongholds;)" (2 Co 10:4).

C. Wiles at a closer look.
   1. The terrifying terror has lost his power and is now the toothless terror.
      a. A strong, healthy lion generally does not roar as he stalks his victim.
      b. Only the toothless lion roars.
      c. He does this to frighten his victim out of his senses. The victim is paralyzed and will injure himself or run right into the old lion.
   2. The tormenting torches can be quenched by the shield of faith or the water of the Word.
   3. The town tough, in reality, is the town bully. Resist him, and he will flee from you.

(Punch him in the nose.) Jesus resisted him in the Word and he fled.

4. The towering towers will become the tottering towers (2 Co 10:5).

D. Wiles are basically a form of nerve (mental) warfare.

1. The roar of the lion in itself cannot hurt anyone. It's designed to scare, intimidate, and frighten.
2. The torches start small fires, which bring distractions of panic, doubt, uncertainty, self-doubt, lust, and self-condemnation.
3. The town bully will run. This perhaps is the area where Satan whips most Christians. He embarrasses them because they give up and become a coward. He insults their manhood, and they lose face.
4. The towering towers are all in the imagination. The method of the devil is to shoot thoughts into the mind, building up the problems while tearing down the self-respect, destroying the self-image, and increasing the inferiority complexes.

E. Wiles can be overcome.

1. Be sober and vigilant. The roar can't hurt you.
2. The shield of faith can quench all the fiery darts.
3. Resist the devil, and he will flee from you.
4. Pull down the strongholds, and bring every thought into captivity.

II. Ways of His Attacks and Ways To Overcome Them – There are seven places where the soul-

winner needs to be sober and vigilant because the adversary will attack him. They are:

A. The Davenport (Sofa).
   1. The devil attacks the soul-winner before he goes soul-winning. He shoots these thoughts into his mind:
      a. I'm so tired.
      b. I've got a headache.
      c. The weather is terrible.
      d. Wouldn't do any good to go anyway.
      e. The deacons don't go, so why should I?
   2. We beat him by taking the shield of faith.
      a. "...faith *cometh* by hearing, and hearing by the Word of God." (Rom. 10:17)
      b. The Word says to go!
      c. "He that observeth the wind shall not sow; and he that regardeth the clouds shall not reap." (Ecc. 11:4)
      d. Go in bad weather. The prospect will think you are either crazy or concerned. The best time to catch people at home is during bad weather.
      e. God will bless your faithful going, especially in bad weather.

B. The door
   1. The soul-winner tenses up and has a big psychological problem at the door. The old lion roars out at him as he stands before the door with fear and trembling.
   2. Overcoming fear at the door

a. It is a psychological impossibility to experience two emotions at the same time.
b. Substitute happiness for fear by thinking of something funny. This will enable you to replace that sickly, little imitation grin for a big, happy smile.
c. God equips the soul-winner for the important task of winning by supplying adrenalin into his system, which will enable him to think clearer and perform at a higher level. Do not mistake this heightening of one's abilities for fear at the door.

C. At the point of dialogue
   1. The devil always attacks after the social visit and before one enters the soul-winning conversation or dialogue.
      a. One has a wonderful social visit. He talks about the nice home, the beautiful little girl, his vocation, etc...
      b. Then his throat gets dry, feels tense, and he can't get into the soul-winning effort.
   2. One beats the devil at the point of dialogue by mastering the five approach questions:
      a. Master the approach questions so well that if one accidentally opens his mouth, the approach questions will pop out.
      b. One has been asking questions that have kept the prospect talking about

himself (SOS). Now it is natural for him to ask the first approach question and thus go right into the soul-winning effort.

D. At the point of decision.
   1. If the devil has only one shot at breaking up or hindering the soul-winning visit, it will be at the point of decision.
      a. The baby will cry.
      b. The prospect will ask a difficult question.
      c. The soul-winner will, for some reason, hesitate, feel insecure, or feel a sense of uncertainty.
   2. Beat the devil at the point of decision by going right to the close.
      a. Tell the prospect you appreciate the privilege of showing him the four spiritual principals, tell him you must leave, but before you go, you would like to have prayer.
      b. Ask him if you may pray... then pray!
      c. Pray for his salvation. Stop the prayer and ask him to take you by the hand if he is willing to accept Christ.
E. At the point of distraction
   1. The devil will distract from the soul-winning visit by using anything or anyone in the environment.
   2. The silent-partner trainee is to create and control the environment so there is a good, healthy atmosphere in which the soul-winner can witness.

3. The main source of distraction will come from the prospect.
    a. The devil will attempt to steal away the seed (Word). (Matt. 13).
    b. The devil will shoot questions or negative thoughts into the prospect's mind (Eph. 6:16).
4. Beat the devil at the point of distraction by "shooing away the birds." One shoos away birds by:
    a. Giving the soul-winners talk in a conversational method instead of through the lecture (monologue) method.
    b. Asking the prospect questions which keeps his mind on the message.
    c. Calling the prospect by name so his mind will focus on your words.
    d. Using gestures which keep the prospect's attention.

F. At the point of duplication
1. A duplicator just mechanically duplicates the same message over and over again. If the devil can intimidate the soul-winner or keep him from perfecting himself in witnessing, then he encourages the soul-winner to witness frequently until the soul talk just becomes a canned talk done mechanically.
2. One overcomes the devil at the point of duplication by realizing:

   a. It's "...Not by might, nor by power, but by my spirit, saith the LORD..." (Zec. 4:6b)
   b. A soul worth Jesus dying for is worth crying for (Psa 126:5).
   c. We are a tray upon which the bread of life is served. Only the Holy Spirit can give life. We must pray and prepare spiritually for soul-winning.
   d. Talk to a lost person just as if he is your closest kin who was and is going to hell.

G. At the point of distortion
   1. The point of distortion is where many great men have lost their power.
      a. King Saul was first humble, but later became proud and self-centered.
      b. King Solomon was first humble, but then became self-sufficient.
      c. The devil begins to tell the soul-winner how great he is. The humble man of God becomes puffed up and begins to have a holier-than-thou attitude and is no longer used of the Lord. He takes the Holy Spirit's credit.
   2. Beat the devil at the point of distortion by realizing:
      a. The Holy Spirit gives the grace. – (2 Cor. 12).
      b. The Holy Spirit gives the wisdom – (Jam. 1:5)

c. The Holy Spirit gives the power – (Acts 1:8)
d. The Holy Spirit is the one who has given all the victories. Do not take His credit. Do not let the devil distort the truth. When we do our best, we are still unprofitable servants. Give the Holy Spirit the praise for His using you and beat the devil.

H. At the point of Discouragement
1. One of the most successful attacks by the Devil **is discouragement**. This was especially true concerning the new people who began to take the great commission seriously.
The Devil is very successful in two areas;
a. Through the disorganization of the visitation outreach
b. **Hindering the new converts from going** to the new evangelistic church. A person wins someone to the Lord who promises to come to church but never does. After returning to his home three or four times to encourage the new convert to come he becomes cold to the soul winner which really discourages the new worker.
2. Disorganization of the Visitation Outreach
a. The most vital way of reaching the community is through organized and trained soul-winning teams. Yet the

average church has **no or a poorly functioning** outreach program.

b. If the average business owner **ran his business as poorly** as the church runs its outreach program it would soon go out of business.

c. Many churches advocate that we are to have world-wide mission program which includes supporting missionaries world-wide as well as trying to reach their community with the gospel. Most members support their world-wide mission program but all but ignore the outreach program. As a result they seldom invite people and most do not go soul-winning. When they do go they find the prospect list is very inadequate which causes them to be assigned to visit the same people **over and over again**. The one in charge of the outreach program gives the devil one of his biggest weapons to defeat and discourage willing workers who soon become discouraged and quit. The answer to the problem could be helped greatly by having **a weekly, well organized visitation service**. (See the ***Designed to Win*** book for more details.) In all my life (of over 60 years visiting in the home weekly) I have never seen a successful visitation program that **didn't** have at least one or more dedicated (church-wide) visitation times a week.

3. Hindering the new convert from going to the new church

   There are basically two main reasons the new convert does not go to the new church:

   - An all-out effort to keep him from going by the devil.
   - They have been taught by Oprah instead of the Bible what being a good Christian is.

4. An all-out effort by the devil to stop the soul-winner from going.

   a. The Bible states "Resist the devil and he will flee from you."This means that the devil is a bully. A bully picks on the young especially those who have not learned how to resist him. In fact most people think those discouraging thoughts which come flooding into their mind are their thoughts when in reality, **the devil shots those thoughts of discouragement and quitting into his mind.**(Eph 6:16) Unless a person is really grounded, the devil will defeat him before he really gets started. He will use every trick in order to keep the new convert from going to the new church.

   b. The first thing which will keep the new soul-winner from quitting is to become aware of the **devil's method of attack.**

c. The second thing a person must be convicted of is that he has been given the **unconditional command to go**. There is not one scripture in the whole Bible that gives a person the **right to quit**.
d. As far as I know, there is only one time that a person asked God how long a person is to keep going. That was in Isaiah chapter six. The answer was, until there are no more people.
e. People are still dying and going to a literal, burning hell where they will weep, and have no peace day or night forever! A child of God has only one decision to make and that is **to be obedient to his Lord, or to be disobedient.**
f. If Jesus hadn't died on the cross in order to pay for our sins, we would have no chance of missing hell. But, He might as well have stayed in heaven **if people never hear of His love and provision**. It is our job to seek them out and tell them. It is the evangelist, pastor and teacher's job **to train and keep the workers motivated**. We must see that older more experienced soul-winners go with and train the new workers.

g. They have been taught by Oprah Winfrey and Hollywood instead of the Bible.
h. We have had fifty years in which many public schools **have had God and the Bible expelled.** They have replaced a personal living God with evolution and humanism. Oprah and the Hollywood crowd teach that in order to be a good Christian, one has only to **go to the church of their choice on Sunday**. A poor lost sinner knows he has sinned, and is afraid that he will go to hell.
i. Along comes a soul-winner and convinces him that he is a sinner and would definitely go to hell. Then the soul-winner reveals to the sinner that the Bible plan of salvation is by grace through faith. In many instances, the sinner is saved or gives every evidence of being saved. Then, the world belief that a person is a good Christian if he goes to the church of his choice once on Sunday takes hold. So that false belief keeps him going to his false church. He actually becomes confused when he is encouraged by the soul-winner to leave his home church (family and friends) and go to a strange church. We either have to do one of two things. **Take more time** with him

before he gets saved in order to convince him that **his false church cannot help him** or his family, or **be grateful** that God has used us to give him the Gospel. After befriending him and encouraging him by making two or three additional visits, we must transfer our time and energy to reach others.

j. I will train – Now that you have committed to being a trainer you will receive great joy by reduplicating yourself by perfecting another trainer.

III. The Wills of Victory – The simple summary of beating the devil at the seven places he attacks the soul-winner are:

A. I will go. – When the devil attacks at the davenport, take the shield of faith and quench his darts and say, "I will go, and then go!"

B. I will smile. – When the devil attacks at the door, think of something funny and say, "I will smile," and then smile!

C. I will share. – When he attacks at the point of dialogue, beat the devil by saying, "I will share," and go into the soul-winning message by asking the five approach questions.

D. I will pray. – When the devil attacks at the point of decision, do not hesitate, go right into the closing. Say to yourself, "I will pray." Next ask the prospect if you may pray, and pray!

E. I will control. – When the devil attacks by using distractions, determine to beat him by resolving, "I will control." Control the conversation and beat the distraction.
F. I will depend upon – When the devil attempts to get you to become mechanical and depend upon yourself, realize that only the Lord can do the conversion and say, "I will depend upon the Holy Spirit to give victory," and you will win.
G. I will acknowledge – Acknowledge your weakness, His great power, His wisdom, His grace, and His achievement, and you will defeat the devil by bearing much fruit.
H. I will train – Now that you have committed to becoming a trainer, you will receive great joy in reduplicating yourself by perfecting another worker.

Summary: The wiles of the devil become the ways of his attacks. The ways of his attacks are by the "I wills" of victory. The "I wills" of victory become the wins for Christ.

1. Quench the fiery darts...
2. Resist the devil...
3. Be sober and vigilant...
4. Pull down the strongholds...

You can beat the devil at his own game!!!!!!!!!!!!!!!

"Beating the Devil at His Own Game!
Lecture Four

1. The wiles of the devil mean his habits or ______________________.
2. If the devil has __________, then ________________ can ____________what they are.
3. The lion roars to _____________ his victim out of __________________.
4. The tormenting ________________ can be ___________________ by the shield of ________________.
5. The towering ________________ (strongholds) will become the ________________ towers.
6. The town ___________ is in reality the town ____________. ________________ him in the nose and he will ______________ from you.
7. The ___________ place the devil attacks the soul-winner is at the _____________.
8. He tries to get the soul-winner to stay ______________ by shooting all types of ______________ into his mind.
9. The second attack is when the lion ____________ at the door which keeps the soul-winner from giving the soul-winning _________________.
10. The point of ______________ is the third place the devil attacks. He does this to keep the soul-winner from giving the soul-winning ________________.
11. The main attack of Satan will come at the _____________of _____________.

12. The point of distraction comes from two sources: the ____________ and the ____________________.
13. The point of duplication is where the soul-winner just ____________ duplicates the same ___________over and over ______________.
14. The point of ____________ is where many great men lost their _____________. They _________________ the Holy Spirit's _________________.

READ THE NOTES OVER ONE TIME, AND IN TWO WEEKS THE AVERAGE PERSON WILL RETAIN ONLY SIX PERCENT. READ THE NOTES OVER EVERY DAY FOR SIX DAYS, AND THE AVERAGE PERSON WILL RETAIN **62%**.

HOW MANY MINUTES OR HOURS DID YOU STUDY YOUR NOTES AND SOUL-WINNING PRESENTATION EACH DAY ON THIS LESSON? WRITE THE AMOUNT OF DAILY TIME AFTER EACH DAY: ONE POINT FOR EACH MINUTE YOU STUDIED. FIFTEEN POINTS FOR EACH DAILY DEVOTION COMPLETED.

Day One___________ Day Two_____________

Day Three__________ Day Four______________

Day Five____________ Day Six______________

TOTAL POINTS _________

NAME____________________________________

Week Four
Daily Devotions

This week's Daily Devotions deals with how to defeat man's greatest enemy, the Devil!
Each Daily Devotion deals with one particular attack of the Devil and how to defeat or overcome that attack.
This makes this one of the most important and beneficial lessons one could ever learn.
Learn these principles and they will help you for the rest of your life!

Lecture Four
Day One
Subject: Birds Seeking the Seed

SCRIPTURE READING: Matthew 13:3-9; 18-23

KEY VERSE: Matthew 13:4, "...some seeds fell...and the fowls came and devoured them..."

PRINCIPLE TAUGHT: When the soul-winning message is presented the devil tries to snatch away the seed. The one presenting the message must learn how to shoo away these birds. The soul-winner can shoo away the birds by:

1. Using the conversational method in presenting the plan of Salvation.
2. Calling the sinner by name.
3. Asking the sinner questions which will keep his mind on what you are saying.
4. Using gestures to illustrate your points.

INDIVIDUAL ACTIVITY: Repeat and discuss the four principles of shooing away birds that are given above.

FAMILY ACTIVITY: Discuss the various ways the devil has in hindering and stealing away the seed in the public services. Does he use such things as passing notes, playing with a baby, whispering, going in and out to the bathroom, etc., etc.?

COMMITMENT PRAYER: Lord, help us to recognize the method the devil uses in distracting the message and then learn to shoo away the birds.

Day Two
Subject: He Shoots His Arrows

SCRIPTURE READING Ephesians 6: 10-18; I John 4:4

KEY VERSE: Ephesians 6:16, "...taking the shield of faith...quench all the fiery darts..."

PRINCIPLE TAUGHT: The method of attack against the child of God comes from the devil through his mind. He shoots flaming darts or arrows of distractions, of doubt, of uncertainty, of self-doubts, of fear, of lust, of passion, and of rebellion. The child of God does not recognize these thoughts for what they are. He associates them to himself which makes him feel like a weak or worthless Christian. Take the Shield of Faith (faith in God's Word) and quench all these harmful thoughts, and have victory over the devil.

INDIVIDUAL ACTIVITY: Fill in the Blanks:

1. Loins girt about with ______________________. Eph. 6:14
2. Having on the breastplate of _______________. Eph. 6:14
3. Feet shod with ________of the gospel of peace. Eph. 6:15
4. Taking the shield of ______________________. Eph 6:16
5. Take the helmet of _______________________. Eph. 6:17
6. The Sword of ____________________________. Eph. 6:18

FAMILY ACTIVITY: Discuss the statement, "Above all, taking the shield of faith...." Does this make faith in God's Word and promises the most important part of the Christians armor?

Day Three
Subject: The Lion Roars

SCRIPTURE READING: I Peter 5:8; I John 4:4; II Tim.1:7

KEY VERSE: I Peter 5:8, "...the devil, as a roaring lion, walketh about..."

PRINCIPLE TAUGHT: The Christian's adversary is pictured as a man-eating lion stalking his victim. The strange thing about this lion is he is pictured as a roaring lion. A roaring lion is generally one who has lost his power and must depend on roaring to confuse, frighten, and cause his victim to become so disconcerted that he will hurt himself or run into the devil's trap. Be sober and vigilant (watchful) means for the child of God to be looking for the devil to roar at him and cause him to become fearful with thoughts of doubt and uncertainty. When this happens, believe the Bible, not your doubts, and have victory over your adversary.

INDIVIDUAL ACTIVITY: Match Statement With Scripture:

1.____	Greater is He that is in you.	A. II Tim. 1:7
2.____	Resist the devil and he will flee.	B. Matt28:18.
3.____	God has not given the spirit of fear.	C. Heb. 13:8
4.____	All power is given unto me.	D. I John 4:4
5.____	Jesus Christ, the same yesterday.	E. James 4:7

FAMILY ACTIVITY: Discuss why a person feels so scared when he goes out witnessing. Who causes the person to have this fear?

Day Four
Subject: The Town Bully Runs

SCRIPTURE READING: James 4:6-8; II Timothy 1:7; I John 4:4

KEY VERSE: James 4:7, "...Resist the Devil, and he will flee from you."

PRINCIPLE TAUGHT: The believer is confronted by the devil who portrays himself as some huge giant who will completely destroy the poor little child of God. Resist the devil (punch him in the nose) and he will flee. He is not as tough as he appears to be but rather a town bully. He will keep whipping you just as long as you allow it. Resist him and you will become, not the victim, but the victor.

INDIVIDUAL ACTIVITY: Match the verses with the words.

1.___ II Timothy 1:7	A. Armour
2.___ Hebrews 10:38	B. Faith
3.___ Matthew 4:4	C. Sound Mind
4.___ Ephesians 6:11	D. Overcometh
5.___ I John 5:4	E. It is Written

FAMILY ACTIVITY: Discuss how the devil shoots thoughts into our minds, gets us to disobey the Lord, and then makes us feel unworthy as a Christian and thus defeats us. How can we overcome and become the victor instead of the victim?

COMMITMENT PRAYER: Lord, teach me to resist the devil and all of his thoughts which cause me to become fearful and disobedient to You.

Day Five
Subject: Pulling Down Strongholds

SCRIPTURE READING: II Cor. 10:5; Eph. 6:16; I John 4:4; II Tim. 1:7

KEY VERSE:

IICorinthians10:4,"...mighty through God to the pulling down of strong holds."

PRINCIPLE TAUGHT: One of the most startling facts in the Bible is presented in verses four and five. The strongholds, which through the Holy Spirit the Christian is to pull down, are nothing more than imaginations. The boogie man is not there. The giants are not there. The great principle here is to believe God and His promises, not the thoughts and imaginations which the devil shoots into ones mind.

INDIVIDUAL ACTIVITY: Match Statement With Scripture:

1.___	Quench all the fiery darts	A. James 4:7
2.___	Pulling down of strongholds	B. Eph. 6:16
3.___	Resist the devil	C. II Cor. 10:4
4.___	Be sober and vigilant	D. I Peter 5:8
5.___	Greater is He that is in you	E. I John 4:4

FAMILY ACTIVITY: Name some problems in the family which may be caused by the devil shooting imaginations into one's mind. Discuss how the devil is able to divide friends; how he divides church members.

COMMITMENT PRAYER: Lord, let me think in a positive Christian way instead of in a negative, suspicious way.

Day Six

Subject: Walking by Faith

SCRIPTURE READING: Matthew 4:1-11; Eph. 6:10-18;I John 4:4

KEY VERSE: I John 4:4, "...greater is he that is in you than he that is in the world."

PRINCIPLE TAUGHT: The child of God has power over the forces of the devil through the Word of God and the ministry of the Holy Spirit. If we stay within the framework of the Bible and allow the Holy Spirit to aid us then we can be victors over the devil every time instead of one of his victims. Greater is He that is in you than he that is in the world.

INDIVIDUAL ACTIVITY: Match Statement with Scripture:

1.___	He shoots the arrows.	A. I Pet. 5:8
2.___	The lion roars.	B. II Cor. 10:4
3.___	Birds seeking the Seed.	C. James 4:7
4.___	The town bully runs.	D. Eph. 6:16
5.___	Pulling down strongholds.	E. Matt. 13:4

FAMILY ACTIVITY: Discuss how the devil attacks the Christian and how the Christian can overcome his attacks.

COMMITMENT PRAYER: Dear Lord, help me to recognize that you have equipped me with spiritual weapons by which I can overcome Satan's attacks.

-Introduction-

Lecture Five
Perfect What You Have, Especially the Closing

Memory Verse

"...let us go on unto perfection..."

Hebrews 6:1

Introduction: The major principles which we have covered in the previous lessons are again reviewed. The continual admonishing of the student to master each principle is strongly stressed.

Remember, just because the seminar is over, it does not mean your effort to master these principles is over.

The Bible absolutely teaches that one is to learn how to soul-win and then train others in soul-winning.

A famous Major League baseball manager used to say "it ain't over until the fat lady sings (referring to the ball game).

THIS SEMINAR "AIN'T" OVER UNTIL YOU STAND BEFORE THE LORD AT THE JUDGMENT SEAT OF CHRIST.

Lecture Five

"Perfect What You Have, Especially the Closing"

Introduction: The curse of the Twentieth Century Christianity is mediocrity!!! Most children of God are satisfied with just getting by. Many are only "lukewarm" and are just halfway doing a job. The Bible commands the Christian to "...go on unto perfection..." God expects you to heed this clear admonition. This command is the basis for our final lesson, "Perfect what you have, especially the closing."

I. **The Bible Teaches Christians to go on to Perfection or Maturity.**

   A. The Bible was written so children of God could be perfected. Paul wrote, "All Scripture is given...: That the man of God may be perfect, throughly [completely] furnished unto all good works" (2 Timothy 3:16-17).

   B. Pastors and evangelists were given to perfect the saints. The Bible states, "And he [God] gave... some, evangelists; and some, pastors and teachers; For the perfecting of the saints..." (Ephesians 4:11-12)

   C. Children of God are commanded to be perfect.

      1. "Be ye therefore perfect, even as your Father...is perfect." (Matthew 5:48).

      2. Bear in mind, the word perfect means to become mature or fully developed—a growth into maturity or godliness. It does not mean sinless perfection.

   D. The Bible promises that the child of God can grow to perfection.

   E. The Christian is commanded to quit playing church and go on to perfection.

II. Perfect What You Have.

In this seminar we have gone over many important principles which we should continue working with until we have perfected them. We should continue to study and rehearse these principles until we have perfected them. We should continue to study and rehearse them – until they become a part of our thinking and daily life.

A. Perfect the fact that you are a fisher of men.
   1. Use the type of bait the fish like as you "fish for men."
   2. Control the conversation by practicing questions which will keep them talking about things in which they are interested.
      S – Self-interest: their family, hobbies, etc.

      O – Occupation: student, homemaker, etc.

      S – Soul-winning effort: religious background.

B. Perfect the fact you are to train other soul-winners.
   1. This means you are to master the principles (2 Timothy 2:2; 1 Peter 3:15)
   2. This means your visitation outreach should be one complete process of training – showing them by doing; teaching them in the public service and from house to house. (Acts 20:20)

C. Perfect the fact you are to walk by faith.
   1. This means you are to harmonize your practice with your theology. Do not fuss at people who misquote the verse, "The just shall walk by faith (sight or feeling)," as if that is the way are going to walk.
   2. Your business is to go. God's business is to bless. He promised if you will go, He will bless (Psalm 126:5-6).

3. Do not look at circumstances or weather, but go! (Eccl 11:4)!
4. Submit yourself to the pastor to be trained, that is, walk by faith, with fear and trembling, until you are a consistent soul-winner-trainer.

D. Perfect the fact that you know the source of your fear.
   1. The devil will roar at you to scare you out of witnessing. Watch for this attack (1 Peter 5:8).
   2. He will insult your manhood – embarrass you by intimidating you into becoming a coward (James 4:7). Punch him in the nose (resist him), and he will flee from you.
   3. He will shoot dirty thoughts into your mind, tear down your self-image, and enlarge your inferiority complex by making you think thoughts of fear, doubt, unworthiness, and lust (Ephesians 6:16).
   4. He will build up impossible situations in your imagination. Bring every thought into captivity, that is, control your thinking. Believe the Bible instead of the devil's lies, which he shoots into your mind (2 Corinthians 10:4-5).

E. Perfect the art of making the proper approach.
   1. Think of something funny before you knock.
   2. Think: "You are the luckiest people in the world. One of God's servants has come to bless you and your house today."
   3. Claim the presence and power of the Holy Spirit.
   4. Go right into the SOS and then the five approach questions.

F. Perfect the fact of "shooing away birds."
   1. Use the conversational method instead of a monologue while witnessing.
   2. Use his name often.

3. Ask him questions which will keep his mind centered on your soul-winning talk.
4. Use gestures to aid his attention.

G. Perfect the method of avoiding questions and the illustration of spiritual truth.

1. When he asks you a question, smile and say, "That is an interesting question. In a little while we will come back to that if you will remind me, but did you notice? Look right here." Then take them right back to the point.
2. They cannot see, perceive, or understand spiritual things (John 3:3). The natural man has no spiritual discernment, so we must use the method Jesus used of illustrating spiritual truth by physical objects. Therefore, perfect the illustrations in the soul-winning talk. This will enhance your chances of getting a genuine conversion instead of a decision.

H. Perfect the fact that you go right into the close by asking him to pray with you.

1. Do not look at or become intimidated by his facial expressions.
2. Let him make his own decision by praying with him and asking him to take your hand if he will accept Christ as his Savior.

III. Perfect The Closing.

A. The most vital time of the soul talk.

1. You are a fisher of men. Jesus said, "...Follow me, and I will make you fishers of men." (Matthew 4:19). "...from henceforth thou shalt catch men." (Luke 5:10). Whoever heard of a fisherman who just fed fish? A good fisherman studies the habits of fish in order to catch fish. That is the sole object of fishing...to catch fish. The most vital time in catching fish is when they bite! A good fisherman gets the fish

committed to the hook when he bites. He knows how to hook the fish, reel him in, and get him safely on the stringer. How is it that some fishermen who fish for men are able to get more of them caught for Jesus than do others who fish for men? There are two main reasons why this is so. Most soul-winners or would be soul-winners need to do serious consideration and work in two areas.

   a. The opening of the soul-winning talk (approach questions), and ...
   b. The closing (the closing is the most vital of the two).

2. Master the closing – One will get so involved in learning the approach questions and the four spiritual principles that he will have a tendency to neglect the closing. Do not overlook the importance of mastering the closing.
3. The soul-winner will reason within himself.
   a. My job is to present the Word.
   b. I don't want to talk him into anything.
   c. I want to make sure his decision is really of the Lord.
   d. You wouldn't reason within yourself that way if there was a burning building and you were trying to rescue a small child from dying in that building, would you? The normal reaction would be to go right into the building if you thought you could save the child. This is what Jude said about saving a person from the eternal fire of hell. Jude 23 states, "...pulling them [rescuing] them out of the fire;..."

   e. Paul talked them into it. "Knowing therefore the terror of the Lord, we persuade men..." (2 Corinthians 5:11). Paul almost persuaded King Agrippa to be saved. The King uttered the heartbreaking words which doomed him to eternal hell in Acts 26:28, "...Almost thou persuadest me to be a Christian" (see also Luke 16:31). We are to persuade men!

4. Negative feedback – If Paul persuaded men and Jude said to snatch (rescue) them, then where did this negative feedback originate? Where does it come from? The devil! The devil shoots these negative thoughts and fears into the soul-winner's mind at the point of decision.
5. The Point of decision – There isn't any other place where the devil attacks any harder than at this vital point of decision.
   a. Silent partner, watch out for that child. He's going to cry or want his mother at the point of decision.
   b. Soul-winner, watch that feeling of insecurity at the point of decision.
   c. Soul-winner, watch that moment of hesitation at the point of decision.
   d. After you have presented a positive, confident image to the prospect in your SOS social visit period through your approach questions and in presenting your four spiritual principles, do not become negative and falter here.
6. Be confident and positive – This is the time the Holy Spirit has waited for. He has hovered over the prospect all of his life for this one moment.

He has kept him alive for this one moment. The Holy Spirit has convicted him for this one moment.

7. The sinner has been looking (in the wrong places) and longing for this one moment. Do not blow this one moment, but be calm and positive. Go right into the closing by saying to the prospect, "Joe, I would like to have a word of prayer. You wouldn't mind if I prayed, would you, Joe?"

B. Twelve proper steps in the closing.

There are twelve simple steps in the closing when the sinner wants to be saved. Twelve may seem to be quite a number for a person to remember, but they are so natural that the soul-winner will not have a problem mastering them. Most people should learn these twelve steps as a silent partner working with a soul-winner in their "on-the-job" training.

1. Ask the sinner to bow his head in prayer.
2. Pray for him. Make the prayer simple, repeat the four spiritual principles, and then pause without saying amen.
3. Ask him to demonstrate his willingness to accept Christ as his Savior by taking your hand.
4. Ask him to repeat a simple prayer.
5. Say, "You really meant that, didn't you, Joe?"
6. Say, "According to the Bible, if you should die right now, where would you go?"
7. Rejoice with him on his salvation.
8. Have him tell someone right then of his salvation.
9. Show him 1 John 5:10-13.

10. Say, "The Holy Spirit wants to use you Joe," and then warn him of the devil and the efforts he will make to keep him from serving God.
11. Make an appointment to pick him up Sunday morning.
12. Have a final prayer with him in which he thanks God for salvation and promises to be in church Sunday.

Summary: Master these principles! Become a fisher of men who is catching men and getting them saved. You will become a fisher of men if you follow Jesus, that is, emulate His life. Perfect what you have, especially the closing.

"Perfect What You Have, Especially the Closing"

Lecture Five

1. The ____________ of modern Christianity is ________________.
2. We are commanded to ______________ ___________ unto ________________.
3. In this seminar, we have gone over many ____________ principles which ____________ should ____________working with until we have ___________ them.
4. Perfect the fact you are to walk by ____________. This means you are to harmonize your ______________ with theology, working with them until we have ____________ them.
5. Most soul-winners need to do ____________ work in two areas. The _________ and the ___________. The ____________ is the most vital of the two.
6. Paul ______________ them into it. "Knowing therefore the terror of the Lord, we ___________ men." (2 Co 5:11)
7. There isn't any other ____________ the devil attacks any ____________ than at the point of _________________.
8. This is the ______________ the Holy Spirit has ______________ for.
9. The sinner has been looking (in the wrong places) and longing for this ________ ________________________.
10. Do not ___________ this one moment, but be calm and ___________. Go right into the closing.

READ THE NOTES OVER ONE TIME, AND IN TWO WEEKS THE AVERAGE PERSON WILL RETAIN ONLY SIX PERCENT. READ THE NOTES OVER EVERY DAY FOR SIX DAYS, AND THE AVERAGE PERSON WILL RETAIN 62%.

HOW MANY MINUTES OR HOURS DID YOU STUDY YOUR NOTES AND SOUL-WINNING PRESENTATION EACH DAY ON THIS LESSON? WRITE THE AMOUNT OF DAILY TIME AFTER EACH DAY: ONE POINT FOR EACH MINUTE YOU STUDIED. 15 POINTS FOR EACH DAILY DEVOTION COMPLETED.

Day One___________ Day Two_____________

Day Three__________ Day Four______________

Day Five____________ Day Six______________

TOTAL POINTS _________

NAME__________________________________

Week Five
Daily Devotions

It is the author's prayer that you have developed a time each day to study the principles which have been covered in the Personal Growth Seminar.

The Daily Devotions found in this week's devotions stress the work of the Holy Spirit. Without His wisdom, grace, power and leadership you will fail.

A wise person will repeat these Daily Devotions until they become part of his thinking and are directing his life.

Lecture Five

Day One

Subject: The Commission

SCRIPTURE READING: Acts 1:8; Luke 24:46-49; John 20:21-23

KEY VERSE: Acts 1:8, "But ye shall receive power...ye shall be witnesses unto me..."

PRINCIPLE TAUGHT: There are five accounts of the great commission found in Matthew, Mark, Luke, John and the Book of Acts. Three of the accounts emphasize the need of divine power. "...tarry ye... until ye be endued with power..." "...he breathed on *them*...receive ye the Holy Ghost." "...ye shall receive power, after that the Holy Ghost is come upon you..."

If you succeed in working for God you must do it through the power of the Holy Spirit. Divine power produces divine results.

INDIVIDUAL ACTIVITY: Match Statement with Scripture:

1.___	preach the Gospel to every creature.	A. Matt. 28:19
2.___	Ye shall receive power after...	B. Mark 16:15
3.___	Receive ye the Holy Ghost	C. Luke 24:29
4.___	Endued with power from on high	D. John 20:22
5.___	Go ye therefore and teach	E. Acts 1:8

FAMILY ACTIVITY: Discuss: Is the Great Commission still in effect today? Is our generation responsible for reaching this generation with the gospel? If the early disciples needed to be filled with the Spirit, do disciples need the filling of the Spirit today?

COMMITMENT PRAYER: Lord, help me be sensitive to Your will for my life and the power, which is available through the Holy Spirit to accomplish that will.

Day Two
Subject: The Challenger

SCRIPTURE READING: Matt. 3:1-12; 11:7-11; Luke 1:80; Luke 1:15; Zech. 4:6

KEY VERSE: Zech. 4:6, "Not by might, nor by power, but by my spirit, saith the LORD of hosts."

PRINCIPLE TAUGHT: The first New Testament preacher was everything a modern day pastor isn't. He was loud, indifferent to people's feelings, ate coarse food, dressed poorly, and lived an isolated life from people, yet he was one of the most successful preachers who ever lived. The secret to his success: he was filled with the Holy Ghost from his mother's womb. His success wasn't in any of his physical liabilities, but in the power of God. God seemed to allow John the Baptist to be the opposite of what most people believe a preacher ought to be in order to emphasize his source of power – filled with the Holy Ghost from his mother's womb. John is an example to us that liabilities can be overcome by a man filled with the Holy Spirit.

INDIVIDUAL ACTIVITY: Fill in the Blanks:

1. Had his raiment of __________ hair. Matt. 3:4
2. His meat was ________ and ______. Matt. 3:4
3. __________ was the Holy Ghost. Luke 1:15
4. Not a risen greater than ______ the Baptist. Matt. 11:11.

FAMILY ACTIVITY: Discuss the need of praying regularly for the Pastor.

Day Three
Subject: The Champion

SCRIPTURE READING: Luke 4:1; Luke 14:21; Acts 10:38

KEY VERSE: Luke 4:1, "And Jesus being full of the Holy Ghost returned from Jordan..."

PRINCIPLE TAUGHT: For thirty years, Jesus was accepted and lived in the midst of His family and friends. When He entered His public ministry, He was filled and empowered by the Holy Spirit. He, as our example, showed us that the proper way to serve is in and through the power of the Holy Spirit.

INDIVIDUAL ACTIVITY: Match Statement with Scriptures:

1.___ Jesus was born in ______________.	A. Luke 4:1
2.___ Jesus talked in the ________.	B. Matt. 2:1
3.___ Jesus was baptized in the _______.	C. Luke 2:46
4.___ Jesus being _______ of the Holy Ghost.	D. Matt. 3:13

FAMILY ACTIVITY: Discuss the subject: Jesus was filled with the Holy Spirit to demonstrate how we can successfully succeed as a Christian.

COMMITMENT PRAYER: Lord, help me see how important it is to be empowered of the Holy Spirit so I can follow the example of Jesus.

Day Four
Subject: The Change

SCRIPTURE READING: Joel 2:28-32; Acts 2:16-21.

KEY VERSE: Acts 2:16,17 "...this is that which was spoken by the prophet Joel; And it shall come to pass in the last days..."

PRINCIPLE TAUGHT: Judges, kings, prophets, and specially chosen servants were the only ones filled with the Holy Spirit in the Old Testament. Joel foresaw the time in which all believers could obtain the power of God in their life. Peter declared that THE CHANGE took place on the day of Pentecost when he said, "THIS IS THAT which was spoken by the prophet Joel..." The same power for all believers is available to this generation, until the sun is darkened and the moon is turned to blood." The fullness of the Spirit is available to every believer today.

INDIVIDUAL ACTIVITY:

1.___ If any of you lack______________.	A. Rom. 5:3
2.___ Ye shall receive ______________.	B. II Cor. 12:9
3.___ My __________ is sufficient.	C. Acts 1:8
4.___ Wait up on the ______... renew.	D. James 1:5
5.___ Tribulation worketh __________.	E. Isa. 40:31

FAMILY ACTIVITY: Discuss the subject: Why the 20th Century Christian is much better off than the Christian who lived in the days of the Old Testament.

Day Five
Subject: The Confusion

SCRIPTURE READING: Acts 1:8; 2:1-11; I Cor. 13:8; I Cor. 14:18-19, 22, 34

KEY VERSE: Acts 2:8, "And how hear we every man in our own tongue, wherein we were born?"

PRINCIPLE TAUGHT: Much confusion prevails in religious circles today concerning the subject of "tongues". Many are asking, "Is speaking in tongues the evidence of being filled with the Spirit or what place do tongues have today if any? What is the unknown tongue?" There are three possibilities, they are:

1. A heavenly language spoken in heaven.
2. An unknown gibberish that no one knows.
3. A known language which is unknown to the speaker.

In Acts2:8 the different nationalities that gathered on the day of Pentecost were startled to hear the Galilaean Jews speaking in the language "wherein we were born." Therefore, the speaking in tongues in the Bible days was the gift of speaking in a known language with the intended design of bringing men to Christ. It has nothing to do with the filling of the Spirit. It was one of the spiritual gifts which was done away when the perfect Bible was completed. The unknown gibberish tongues of today are not the same as the gift of language in the Bible days and brings confusion to MANY who are SEEKING to be filled with the Spirit as the Bible commands.

Day Six
Subject: The Command

SCRIPTURE READING: Eph. 5:18; Luke 11:13; Acts 5:32

KEY VERSE: Ephesians 5:18, "...And be not drunk with wine wherein is excess; but be filled with the spirit."

PRINCIPLE TAUGHT: There are many commands in the Bible. One of the plainest to the child of God is for him to be filled with the Spirit. There is NO WAY to explain away this direct command – to be filled with the Holy Spirit. It is a command that is obeyed or disobeyed. It is for this generation ... it is for you.

INDIVIDUAL ACTIVITY: Match Statement With Scripture:

1. ___	Be filled with the Spirit	A. Acts 1:8
2. ___	Ye shall receive power	B. Luke 1:15
3. ___	Filled from his mother's womb	C. Acts 2:8
4. ___	Where in we were born	D. Luke 4:1
5. ___	Jesus being full of the Holy Ghost	E. Eph. 5:18

FAMILY ACTIVITY: Discuss: Is it right for a child of God to get drunk? Is it right for a child of God to ignore the command to be filled with the Spirit?

COMMITMENT PRAYER: Lord, help me to empty myself of any selfishness and worldliness so you can fill me with thy Spirit.

SALVATION

MAKE YOUR CALLING AND ELECTION SURE.

MAKE SURE YOU ARE A CHRISTIAN! This verse teaches that the believer has part in his election (salvation). The first thing a person needs to do in order to properly worship God is to make sure he knows Him. If one isn't SURE, he can make his "...calling and election sure..." by turning from his sin, and calling upon the name of the Lord for Salvation. (II Peter 1:10)

The following outline of the dialogue is the one used in the training during the seminar.

Saved for Certain

"...that ye may know that he have eternal life..." I John 5:13.

Let us re-examine the Four Spiritual Principles. This will help you realize the fullness of the decision you made in accepting Jesus as your Savior.

THE FIRST SPIRITUAL PRINCIPLE IS THE FACT OF SIN:

"For all have sinned and come short of the glory of God;".(Romans 3:23)

1) The word, "ALL", places us "ALL IN THE SAME BOAT."
   This means that I have sinned. It means the finest person in the world has sinned. It means "YOU" have sinned also.
2) YOU HAVE HEARD OF THE TEN COMMANDMENTS, HAVEN'T YOU?

Most people are trying to keep the Ten Commandments and by doing so, they hope to go to heaven when they die! In reality every normal adult has broken most, if not all, of these commandments. For example,

a) One of the commandments states, "Thou shalt not take the name of the LORD thy God in vain, [or swear]..."
b) Another says, "Honor thy Father and Mother."
c) Still a third states, "Thou shalt not bear false witness [or lie]."

3) ILLUSTRATION TO HELP YOU SEE THAT ALL HAVE SINNED.

May I ask you this question? HOW MANY BANKS would a man have to rob before he became a bank robber? By the same logic, one lie would make a person a liar, while one sin would make a person a sinner.

THE SECOND SPIRITUAL PRINCIPLE IS THE CONSEQUENCES OF SIN:

"For the wages of sin *is* death..." (Romans 6:23)

1) THERE ARE TWO KEY WORDS IN THIS VERSE, WAGES AND DEATH.

Wages means a payoff, penalty or what one gets for being a sinner. Death means separation.

2) HAVE YOU EVER BEEN TO A FUNERAL?

The body is lying there in a casket. The real person has been separated from his body. This is physical death.

3) WHEN YOU DIE GOD WANTS TO REACH RIGHT DOWN AND TAKE YOU RIGHT INTO HEAVEN.

But, if you are still in your sins, have never been reconciled, born again, or saved; God will say to you, "Your sins separate you from me, your sins shut you out of heaven."

4) THERE ARE ONLY TWO ETERNAL PLACES.

One is heaven, where God is, and the other is hell a literal place of fire, pain, and separation. The wages, or pay off for being a sinner is eternal separation from God in hell.

THE THIRD SPIRITUAL PRINCIPLE IS THE REMEDY FOR SIN:

"But God commendeth his love toward us, in that, while we were yet sinners, Christ died for us." (Romans 5:8)

1) GOD HAS THIS PROBLEM TO SOLVE.

You acknowledged that you were a sinner and the Bible states that if you pay for your sin, then you will be separated from God eternally in hell. How can God send you to hell, and at the same time take you to heaven?

2) TO ILLUSTRATE THIS PROBLEM

Let me ask you this question. "HOW CAN I BE IN TWO PLACES AT THE SAME TIME?" You say, "You can't be." God had to work out how you could pay for your sin by dying (going to hell) and yet be forgiven, and go to heaven. IT SEEMED IMPOSSIBLE! His solution! If someone would die in your place and pay for your sins, then God would forgive you and take you to heaven for that person's sake.

3) THAT'S WHAT JESUS WAS DOING ON THE CROSS. He was dying as a substitute, paying for your sins " Christ died for you" or in your place.

4) LET ME ASK YOU, "HAVE YOU EVER RECEIVED A TRAFFIC TICKET?"

Imagine that I received a traffic ticket, appeared before the judge, who pronounced judgment upon me by saying, "It will take $25.00 or five days in jail to satisfy the State of Texas." If I did not have any money and could not pay my fine, the State of Texas would still be satisfied if someone else paid this ticket for me. THAT IS WHAT JESUS DID ON THE CROSS FOR YOU. He was paying your SIN TICKET, satisfying THE LAW OF GOD which demanded payment.

PERSONAL APPLICATION:

Before going on to the final Spiritual Principle let us reason. According to Romans 3:23 you realize that you are a ____________. In Romans 6:23 God said that the ______ of sin is ______ or eternal separation from God. That means that if a person pays for his own sins he will go to ______. But in Romans 5:8 you realize that "God ____________ his love toward us [you]..." and has given His ______ on the cross in your place, and paid for your ______.

THE FOURTH SPIRITUAL PRINCIPLE IS THE INDIVIDUAL RESPONSE:

"For whosoever shall call upon the name of the Lord shall be saved." (Romans 10:13)

1) THERE ARE TWO KEY WORDS IN THIS VERSE.

They are WHOSOEVER and SAVED (from hell). WHOSOEVER means you! It means anyone who calls upon the name of the Lord. Jesus died and paid the sin debt for every man. The word SAVED means delivered from hell.

2) "SHALL CALL UPON" MEANS, PRAY OR ASK.

This verse says, "If you really understand that you are a sinner, that you are going to hell; that Jesus literally died in your place (paid for your sin), and that if you call upon the name of the Lord, and ASK Him to save you for Jesus sake, HE WILL SAVE YOU FROM HELL.

3) JESUS AND HIS FATHER REACHED THIS AGREEMENT.

If Jesus died in your place and paid for your sin, then God, the Father, would accept His death as full payment for your sins and save you from Hell – if you would ask Him to save you for Jesus' sake. In heaven, Jesus is seated beside His Father, reminding Him of this agreement and pleading the sinners case right now. He is saying, "I died for him. I paid for his sin, now FORGIVE HIM AND SAVE HIM FOR MY SAKE." God will honor His word and save every sinner who turns from his sin, and earnestly desires and asks for the forgiveness of sin. If you haven't already done so – bow your head and pray this simple prayer right now. "Dear Lord, I acknowledge my sin. I accept you as my Lord and Saviour. From this day on, I will live for you In Jesus' name Amen.

PERSONAL APPLICATION

I, ______________________, do now accept Jesus Christ as my personal Savior. From this day, ______________________, I will trust Him and live for Him.

I NOW HAVE THE WITNESS WITHIN

In I John 5:10 the Bible proclaims, "He that believeth on the Son of God hath the witness[knowledge or testimony] in himself. he that believeth not hath made Him a liar..." God puts the individual on the spot. He either believed and was saved or he called God a liar. If one believed and trusted Christ as his Savior, he was the witness, or testimony, within himself.

PERSONAL APPLICATION

I, _________________________, sitting in my home or______________________ (write down place) have the inner knowledge that I have received Jesus Christ as my personal Saviour.

In verse eleven, it says, "...this is the record that God has given to us **eternal life**[never ending life]." In verse twelve he says, "he that hath [received] the Son hath life [eternal life]." In verse thirteen He boldly states, "...ye may **know**[not guess or hope] that ye **have**[not will have if you hold out faithfully to the end] **eternal life**..." These verses simply state that you are saved and you know for certain that you are saved.